NAMES
FOR
MUSLIM CHILDREN

BY
MOULANA RAFEEQ HATHURANI

Islamic Book Service (P) Ltd.

Published with the Permission of **Islamic Promotions**
P.O.Box-289, Crown Mines-2025, R.S.A.

Names For Muslim Children

by **Moulana Rafeeq Hathurani**

ISBN 81-7231-034-X
Reprint: 2012

Published by:

Islamic Book Service (P) Ltd.

1511-12, Pataudi House, Darya Ganj, **New Delhi**-110002 **(INDIA)**
Tel.: +91-11-23253514, 23269050, 23286551, 23244556, 64637515
Fax: +91-11-23277913, 23247899 | **E-mail:** islamic@eth.net
Website: www.ibsbookstore.com

Our Associates

- Al-Munna Book Shop Ltd. **(U.A.E.)**
  (Sharjah) ***Tel.:*** 06-561-5483, 06-561-4650
  (Dubai) ***Tel.:*** 04-352-9294
- Azhar Academy Ltd., **London (United Kingdom)**
  Tel.: 020-8911-9797
- Lautan Lestari (Lestari Books), **Jakarta (Indonesia)**
  Tel.: 0062-21-35-23456
- Husami Book Depot, **Hyderabad (India)**
  Tel.: 040-6680-6285

Printed in India

CONTENTS

Translation of

Foreword

Psychologists now apprehend the wisdom of the effect a person's name has on his life. But Muhammad (sallallaahu-alayhi-wasallam) had revealed this fact to his followers already 1400 years ago. His teaching to his followers was that children should be given good names, and that meaningless names and those having unsavoury connotations should be avoided. Subsequently, we find many incidents mentioned in the Hadith where Rasoolullah (sallallaahu-alayhi-wasallam) changed the names of people with this object.

Another aspect of a person's name is that it bespeaks a person's religion. Hence the name of a Muslim is usually of such a nature that by the mere mention of it, the listener understands that the person so addressed, is a Muslim. It is for this reason that our elders laid great emphasis on keeping good and pleasant names.

But since the widespread of Western culture throughout the world, it has become customary amongst Muslims not to take into congnisance the meaning of the name when naming a child. Many do not even bother to ascertain whether it is permissible for one to keep such a name or not. Often, even if the name is correct and suitable, then by way of abbreviating it, its Islamic connotation is distorted. In fact, at times it even become unlawful to address one by such a name. For example, Abdur-Rahmaan is called Rahmaan; Abdur-Razzaaq, Razzaaq; Abdul-Wahhaab, Wahhaab-whereas Rahmaan, Razzaaq and Wahhaab are the exclusive epithets of Allah Ta'ala. To address any creation by such a name, is therefore unlawful.

While this disease is rampant in the entire Muslim World, it is more in vogue in South Africa: Sulaimaan is called Solly; Yoosuf is called Joosub, Essop or Joe; Uthmaan is called Ozman etc. In this way the blessed names of the Ambiyaa' (alayhimus-salaam) and Sahaabad (radhiyallaahu-anhum) are distorted and needlessly rendered meaningless. Moreover, one may never know whether the one so addressed is a Muslim or not.

Hence, with regard naming children, there was a need for compiling a book wherein all misconceptions could be eradicated and guidance could be given as to the importance of giving correct and meaningful names. Alhamdolillah, respected brother, Molana Qaree Muhammad Rafeeq, teacher at Madrasah Islamia, Lenasia has fulfilled this need proficiently in the pages to follow. The respected compiler has in his introduction explained most ably the Islamic teachings regarding a new-born child. The Masaa'il pertaining to Tahneek, Azaan, Duaas, circumcision, naming a child—and many more—have been explained in detail. Apart from having compiled a book on Muslim names in an alphabetic order, he has also rendered their meanings and their literal and historical aspects as well. During my tour of South Africa, I have had a cursory perusal of the book from various portions and found it to be most invaluable. In my opinion it should find its place into the home of every Muslim—that no family should remain without it.

May Allah grant the compiler the best of rewards in both the worlds for the services rendered by him, and may He also grant this book acceptance and grant him the guidance to render more and greater service of this nature. Ameen.

Azaadville, Krugersdorp
South Africa.

Muharram, 1401

Muhammad Taqee Uthamani
Servant of the Students

Darul-Uloom, Karachi

INTRODUCTION

بِسْمِ اللّٰهِ الرَّحْمٰنِ الرَّحِيْمِ. اَلْحَمْدُ لِلّٰهِ الْقَائِلِ فِىْ كِتَابِهِ الْمُبِيْنِ . وَلَا تَنَابَزُوْا
بِالْاَلْقَابِ. بِئْسَ الِاسْمُ الْفُسُوْقُ بَعْدَ الْاِيْمَانِ . وَمَنْ لَّمْ يَتُبْ فَاُولٰئِكَ هُمُ
الظّٰلِمُوْنَ . وَنَشْهَدُ اَنْ لَّا اِلٰهَ اِلَّا اللّٰهُ وَاَنَّ مُحَمَّدًا عَبْدُهٗ وَرَسُوْلُهٗ . اَللّٰهُمَّ
صَلِّ عَلٰى سَيِّدِنَا مُحَمَّدٍ وَّعَلٰى آلِ سَيِّدِنَا مُحَمَّدٍ وَّعَلٰى اَصْحَابِ سَيِّدِنَا
مُحَمَّدٍ وَّبَارِكْ وَسَلِّمْ. اَمَّا بَعْدُ . قَالَ اللّٰهُ تَبَارَكَ وَتَعَالٰى فِىْ كِتَابِهِ
الْكَرِيْمِ. اَلْيَوْمَ اَكْمَلْتُ لَكُمْ دِيْنَكُمْ وَاَتْمَمْتُ عَلَيْكُمْ نِعْمَتِىْ وَرَضِيْتُ لَكُمُ
الْاِسْلَامَ دِيْنًا .

Allah Ta'ala says in the Holy Qur'aan:
Today I have perfected for you your religion and have completed my favour upon you, and have chosen for you Islaam as your religion.
. . . Ma'idah.

Verily the religion with Allah (true, genuine and acceptable by Allah) is Islaam. *. . . Aale-Imraan.*

In the first-mentioned verse Allah Ta'ala refers to Islaam as a "perfect" and "complete" religion which Allah Ta'ala has "chosen" for us. In the second verse He has referred to it as the "only" religion acceptable by Him. Since Islaam is as mentioned by Allah Ta'ala, it is the bounden duty of every Muslim to ensure the upbringing of his children in strict Islaamic fashion—with an attitude of total indifference to the cultures and fashions concocted by the West . . . with which even the West today has become disillusioned and disenchanted.

The choice is entirely ours: either we rear children who will be a credit to their *Deen*, comfort to their families and a boon to society; or by slavishly adhering to the trash passed of as "modern" and "fashionable," we will reap untold heartbreak when these children, after reaching adolescence, prove rebellious and disobedient for both, their families and society at large.

If we are desirous of children imbued with true Islaamic spirit then we must mould our lives strictly in accordance with the *nooraani* teachings of our beloved Rasool *sallallaahu-alayhi-wasallam* so that from the very beginning of conception, our children will be blessed with the *noor* and true spirit of Islaam.

In the pages to follow in this introduction we shall endeavour to present to you a mere cursory reflection of what the Religion of Islaam has to offer to us in paving our way towards eternal *falaah* and salvation.

THE EXPECTANT MOTHER . . . ADVICE TO HER

It is irrefutable that the mother's proper nourishment has a telling effect on the health of the yet-to-be-born child. In the like manner the spiritual nourishment of the mother is no less important. If the mother is desirous of an obedient, pious and spiritually healthy child–and which Muslim parent isn't?– she has no choice but to think and act in a manner which will manifest the luminous spirit of Islaam. She will have to spend much time offering her devotions to Allah by performing *salaat*, making *dhikr*, reciting the Holy Qur'aan etc. This will have a two-fold result: the mother will remain spiritually and mentally healthy and at the same time the child will be inherritting piety, good manners and many other angelic qualities–*insha-Allah.*

It is no wonder then that these angelic qualities are often manifested in the infancy of many a great personality. It is said of some Auliyaa-Allah that they were born with certain portions of the Holy Qur'aan already imprinted in their memory. Others even refused to drink the milk of their mother during the holy month of Ramadaan.

Here is an authentic incident mentioned in the Bukhari and Muslim to substantiate that the acts of virtue of parents certainly have positive effects on their progenies for generations to come.

Aboo Talhah (RA), a companion of Rasoolullah *sallallaahu-alayhi-wasallam*, had a son who had fallen gravely ill. During that period the father had to leave home for a number of days on an important errand, leaving the child to the care of the mother. Whilst away, the sickness caused the death of the child.

The mother beseeched the people not to inform her husband even when he returned. When he returned his very first enquiry was about his son. She answered that he (their son) is presently in a more comfortable state than that which he had been in . . . meaning that death had rendered him peace and comfort. By this answer the husband understood that he had recuperated. She then offered him his supper which he ate with relish. The good wife then even adorned herself as best she could which filled him with passionate feelings. When she saw that his needs had been tended to then only did she disclose to him the death of their son. This stark news proved a severe blow to him. He was annoyed and overcome with intense grief . . . that she had not disclosed to him the child's fate earlier, and, instead allowed him to perform an act which necessitates *ghusl.*

At daybreak he approached Rasoolullah *sallallaahu-alayhi-wasallam* and related to him what had transpired during the night. Rasoolullah *sallallaahu-alayhiwasallam* intently asked him whether they had copulated. When he answered in the affirmative, he blessed them by saying: "O Allah, grant them blessings for what had transpired during the night." A male issue was born of them whose *Tahneek* was done by Rasoolullah *sallallaahu-alayhi-wasallam*. He named him "Abdullah". When Abdullah grew up and married, Allah Ta'ala blessed him with nine children, all of whom became *huffaaz* of the Holy Qur'aan and learned *ulamaa* of their time. This overwhelming attainment can only be attributed to the acts of virtue of the grand-mother of these *ulamaa.*

It becomes apparent from the above incident that acts of virtue of parents not only have a telling effect on their children but also on their progenies for generations to come.

WHEN A CHILD IS BORN . . .

It is indeed a joyous occasion when parents are blessed with a child. However, the extent of the joy could be enhanced even further if the laws of Shariat are adhered to and all other meaningless rituals are cast aside since they are neither mentioned in the Holy Qur'aan nor cited in the Hadeeth.

After birth the child should be given proper *ghusl*. Thereafter the message of the Greatness and Oneness of Allah Ta'ala, and the prophethood of Rasoolullah *sallallaahu-alayhi-wasallam* should be the first words to reach the child's innocent ears. This should be accomplished by giving *azaan* near his right ear and *iqaamat* close to his left. This noble task should be the prerogative of an *aalim* or a pious elder of the family. If such a person is not at hand then any Muslim male may perform this *sunnah*.

DU'AAS ON THIS BLESSED OCCASION

It is *mustahab* to recite the following *du'aa* after the *azaan* and *iqaamat*:

اَللّٰهُمَّ اِنِّىْ أُعِيْذُهَا بِكَ وَذُرِّيَّتَهَا مِنَ الشَّيْطَانِ الرَّجِيْمِ

O Allah, I seek your protection for her and her decendants from the cursed Shaytaan.

Note: For boys read: أُعِيْذُهُ and وَذُرِّيَّتَهُ

بِسْمِ اللّٰهِ الرَّحْمٰنِ الرَّحِيْمِ . قُلْ هُوَ اللّٰهُ أَحَدٌ . أَللّٰهُ الصَّمَدُ . لَمْ يَلِدْ وَلَمْ يُوْلَدْ . وَلَمْ يَكُنْ لَّهُ كُفُوًا اَحَدٌ .

In the name of Allah, most Beneficient, most Merciful. Say! He is Allah, the One. Allah is one on whom depends the entire creation and He depends on no one. He begetteth not, nor is He begotten. And there is none akin to Him.

اَللّٰهُمَّ اجْعَلْهُ بَرًّا تَقِيًّا . وَاَنْبِتْهُ فِى الْاِسْلَامِ نَبَاتًا حَسَنًا .

For girls read:

اَللّٰهُمَّ اجْعَلْهَا بَرَّةً تَقِيَّةً وَاَنْبِتْهَا فِى الْاِسْلَامِ نَبَاتًا حَسَنًا .

O Allah, make him/her pious and Godfearing and let him/her grow up in Islaam to his/her excellent growth.

اَللّٰهُمَّ عَلِّمْهُ الْكِتَابَ وَالْحِكْمَةَ وَفَقِّهْهُ فِى الدِّيْنِ .

For girls read:

اَللّٰهُمَّ عَلِّمْهَا الْكِتَابَ وَالْحِكْمَةَ وَفَقِّهْهَا فِى الدِّيْنِ ۔

O Allah, teach him/her the Qur'aan and wisdom and give him/her the understanding in Deen.

TAHNEEK

Tahneek means the placing of a piece of date, softened by chewing, on the palate of the new-born. The practice of *tahneek* is *masnoon* since Rasoolullah *sallallaahu-alayhi-wasallam* made the *tahneek* of Abdullah bin Zubair (RA) and Abdullah bin Talhah (RA). Unfortunately this practice of *tahneek* is rarely acted upon in modern times. The reward of reviving a 'dying' *sunnah* of Rasoolullah *sallallaahu-alayhi-wasallam* is boundless. Here again, this should be the prerogative of a learned *aalim* or a pious elder of the family. Otherwise any Muslim male would suffice. If dates are not available, honey should serve as an ideal substitute.

PRECAUTION AGAINST MISFORTUNE

In order to safeguard children against misfortune, the following *du'aa* should be recited as often as possible and 'blown' on the child:

اَعُوْذُ بِكَلِمَاتِ اللّٰهِ التَّامَّاتِ مِنْ شَرِّ كُلِّ شَيْطَانٍ وَّهَامَّةٍ وَّمِنْ شَرِّ كُلِّ عَيْنٍ لَامَّةٍ

I seek protection by the perfect words of Allah from the evil of every devil and reptile, and from the evil of every revengeful eye.

Aayatul-Kursi and the four *Quls* may also be recited and "blown" on the child.

THE AFTERBIRTH AND NAVAL-CORD

The afterbirth and naval-cord should be buried with due care since they are portions of the human body. As such, it should be treated with respect and honour. Disposing it in the drain or garbage is contrary to this concept. It is for this reason, too, that the dead body of a human being may not be cremated or abandoned in a pit for vultures and other animals to devour it...as is customary among the people of other religions.

FEEDING

As the infant is the offspring of its mother it is common knowledge that the mother's milk is the most suitable source of nourishment for the baby. Therefore, the mother should most obligingly fulfil her duty of breast-feeding the child. By so doing bonds of love, affection and intimacy are strengthened between mother and child, and in the process, good habits and character are transmitted to the child. All these and countless other benefits are contained in breast-feeding. Artificial methods of feeding are all devoid of these advantages. Other methods of feeding should only be resorted to if ill health or other circumstances do not permit her to breast-feed the child. However, she must ensure that no *haraam* food is consumed by the child. *Bismillah* should always be recited before feeding.

MAXIMUM PERIOD FOR BREAST-FEEDING

The maximum period for which a child could be breast-fed is two years. To exceed this period is not permissible since the use of any part of the human body, *without necessity*, is not allowed. The milk of the mother is portion of the human body and there is *no necessity* to feed the child for more than two years. Therefore not to wean the child after the permissible period is *haraam.*

THE CHILD'S ATTIRE.

Muslim males may not adorn themselves with clothes of silk or any red and bright orange (saffron) colour. Neither gold nor silver ornaments. Adornment is characteristic of womanhood.

Parents should also ensure that children dress in an honourable and modest manner–never immitating the ostentatious styles that may be in vogue. Due to the incorrect concept of 'freedom' and 'broad-mindedness', parents allow their children to dress and act in a manner they wish. This eventually results in problematic, rebellious and disobedient children who in adolescent stages cause parents and society untold heartbreak and much anxiety.

HAIR, AQEEQAH AND NAMING THE CHILD

It is *mustahab* to remove the baby's hair and to observe the *aqeeqah* and to name the child on the seventh day after birth. Gold or silver equivalent to the weight of the removed hair may be given as charity to the poor. Otherwise its equivalent value in money. The hair, being a portion of the human body should be buried with due respect. *Aqeeqah* is a form of *sadaqah* whereby the child is safeguarded against misfortunes. Two sheep or two goats are offered for a boy while one goat or sheep suffices for a girl. If the seventh day co-incides with the days of *qurbaani* then portions of a cow, ox or camel may be offered as *qurbaani* and portions as *aqeeqah*.

KHATNAH OR CIRCUMCISSION

Circumcission before seven years is *mustahab*. The baby's health must be taken into consideration before deciding on *khatnah*. However, *khatnah* before he attains twelve years is imperative.

WHEN THE CHILD BEGINS TO TALK

The child should first be taught to say the *kalimah* when he begins to talk:

لَا إِلٰهَ إِلَّا اللّٰهُ مُحَمَّدٌ رَّسُوْلُ اللّٰهِ

EDUCATION AND GOOD MANNERS

Islaam lays considerable emphasis on education and good character. It is the children's rightful claim to be given sound Islaamic education and taught good manners. This will not only afford the children happiness in both the worlds, but they will prove great assets to both, their families and society as well. This is why Rasoolullah *sallallaahu-alayhi-wasallam* declared good manners as the 'best thing' a father can impart to his children. He also declared the mother as the 'shepherdess' of the household which implies that she is responsible for the correct upbringing of her children.

WHAT PARENTS OWE THEIR CHILDREN

1. SELF-ESTEEM: Parents owe their children personal worth and self-esteem which are the cornerstones for sound mental health. A child who is constantly criticized, "put down", reproached, made to feel stupid and inept, continually compared with brothers or cousins who do better, will become so unsure and so terrified that he or she will lose enthusiasm for learning and becoming successful.

2. PRAISING THE CHILD AND EXPRESSING LOVE: A child needs to be praised every now and again for his achievements and good behaviour. Some parents find it difficult to voice their approval or praise the child. However, there are other modes of expressing approval as well—a smile, caress or a kiss will convey approval. All these acts of love are very essential for producing children who are healthy in mind and body. It is for this reason that our Shari'ah lays considerable stress on showing love and affection to children. Rasoolullah *sallallaahu-alayhi-wasallam* said that one who does not have mercy on our children and does not respect our elders, is not from among us.

3. EQUALITY: Parents should always treat their children equitably. Children tend to grow miserable, lose confidence, become discouraged and resentful if parents show favoritism towards a particular child. It is related by Hadhrat Aa'i'shah (RA) that once she offered a date to a lady beggar who was accompanied by her two daughters. The lady shared the date between her two daughters, depriving herself of a share. Then she departed. When Rasoolullah *sallallaahu-alayhi-wasallam* came home, she related to him the incident. He said: "Whoever is "involved" with any daughters, and he treats them well (equitably), this will serve as a protection for him from the Fire."

4. BASIC ISLAMIC EDUCATION: It is the duty of every parent to ensure that his children have basic Islamic education which covers *aqaa'id* or Islamic beliefs, the five principles of Islaam, the rules and *masaa'il* pertaining to these five principles and the correct recital of the Holy Qur'aan.

5. STANDARDS AND VALUES: Decent standards and solid values should also be taught to the child. This means being respectful to parents, elders, the Ulama, teachers and just laws.

CLEANLINESS AND OTHER NECESSARY PRECAUTIONS

Sharia't has termed cleanliness half of *Imaan*. As such the mother should personally accomplish all maternal devotions such as feeding, bathing and keeping the child clean and *'paak.'* Soiled clothes must be cleaned without delay so that the danger of bacteria spreading is nipped in the bud. Thus, *barakah* and happiness will abound. The baby should also be immunized against infantile diseases. This does not, however, imply lack of faith and reliance in Allah.

NAMING THE CHILD

It is the infant's vested right to be honoured with a good name. When choosing a name for the child, it should be done with the intention that the child will be blessed with the *barakah* of that name. Here are some *Ahadeeth* to show the importance of selecting a good and correct name:

> Ibne Umar (RA) relates Rasoolullah *sallallaahu-alayhi-wasallam* as saying: "Truly, the most loved of your names by Allah are *Abdullah* and *Abdur-Rahmaan*."
>
> It is also reported in the Aboo Dawood that Rasoolullah *sallallaa-hu-alayhi-wasallam* said: "Keep the names of prophets. And the most desirable names by Allah Ta'ala are *Abdullah* and *Abdur-Rahmaan*. And names that depict honesty are *Haarith** and *Hammaam.** And the most disliked ones are *Harb** and *Murrah.*"*

THE BARAKAH OF NAMING A CHILD AFTER THE BELOVED NAME OF RASOOLULLAH (sallallahu-alayhi-wasallam)

Rasoolullah *sallallaahu-alayhi-wasallam* said: "Whoever is named after me with the hope of being blessed, he will be blessed and will be in peace till the Day of Qiyaamah."

He also said: "To whomever is born a boy and he names him *Muhammad* solely for the love of me and for the blessings of my name, then both he (the father) and his son will enter Jannah."

THE IMPORTANCE OF KEEPING GOOD NAMES

HADEETH: "On the Day of Qiyaamah you will be called by your (own) names and the names of your fathers. Therefore keep good names." Aboo Dawood.

HADEETH: "To whomever is born a child, the child should be given a good name and sound education. And when he becomes of age he should be married."

*Haarith: planter; Hammaam: thoughtful; Harb: battle; Murrah: bitter.

It was Rasoolullah's *sallallaahu-alayhi-wasallam* practice to enquire the names of persons and villages. If they were pleasant, it became apparent on his face. If not, his displeasure could be seen.

Once Rasoolullah *sallallaahu-alayhi-wasallam* called for a volunteer to milk a camel. Four persons volunteered: he refused to accept the services of the first three because their names did not imply pleasantness. The names of the first two were *Murrah* (bitter) while *Jamrah* (burning coal) was the name of the third person. When the fourth said his name is *Ya'eesh* (long live) Rasoolullah *sallallaahu-alayhi-wasallam* said to him: "Milk her."

UNDESIRABLE NAMES SHOULD BE CHANGED

Aa'ishah (RA) reports that Rasool *sallallaahu-alayhi-wasallam* used to change displeasing names replacing them with good names.

Abdullah bin Umar (RA) relates that one of his sisters was named *Aasiyah* (عاصية disobedient). Rasoolullah *sallallaahu-alayhi-wasallam* changed it to *Jameelah* (جميلة beautiful).

Zainab (RA) says that I had been named *Birrah* (برة pious). Rasoolullah *sallallaahu-alayhi-wasallam* said: "Do not claim piety for Allah knows best who amongst you are pious. Name her *Zainab*!"

NAMES MAY INFLUENCE THE LIVES OF PEOPLE

Sa'eed ibne Musaiyib (RA) relates from his father that his grandfather went to Rasoolullah *sallallaahu-alayhi-wasallam* and was asked: "What is your name?" He replied: "Hazn" (sorrow). Rasoolullah *sallallaahu-alayhi-wasallam* said: "You are Sahl." (contended). He replied: "I will not change the name my father had given me." The narrator says that thereafter sorrow continually remained with them.

KEEP AWAY FROM NAMES IMPLYING SHIRK

As Muslims, we should always abstain from keeping names implying any elements of Shirk, like adjoining the word 'Abd' (عبد servant) to names or epithets other that those of Allah Ta'ala.

Rasoolullah *sallallaahu-alayhi-wasallam* also forbade keeping pompous and self-glorifying names, for this reveals arrogance and haughtiness—human elements most abhorred by Allah Ta'ala.

BE PROUD OF YOUR IDENTITY AND FAITH

Muslims should always be proud of their identity and faith. Nowadays, to conceal his identity, it is common practice for a person to 'westernize' his name, like substituting Yoosuf with Joe or Joseph, Sulaimaan with Solly or Sully, Faatimah with Fatli, Sumay-yah with Summi etc. Efforts to distort such beautiful names merely reveal an un-Islamic and sacreligious attitude.

Remember, there exists behind each Islamic name an Islamic spirit and meaning, which, when distorted, is ruined. For example, there is intended love for the Prophet of Islam, and *barakah* when naming a child *Muhammad*. But when *Muhammad* is called *Mahmad* or *Gammat*, this spirit of love for Rasoolullah *sallallaahu-alayhi-wasallam* and the acquiring of *barakah* by such a name is shattered. Should we not then refrain from such sacreligious practices?

May Allah Ta'ala guide us so that we may realize the beauty and uniqueness of the religion of Islam propounded by no other than the one who is the best of Allah's creations–May Allah shower His choicest blessings upon him.

May Allah Ta'ala guide us on the Right Path.

May He also grant this humble effort of mine to be a fulfilment of a long-felt need amongst the Muslims–especially the English-speaking Muslims. Ameen.

The Compiler,
M. Rafeeq

MORE ABOUT MEANINGLESS NAMES . . . which Muslims should not keep.

It is common practice in our society to keep names having no meaning at all. Consider the following words used as names. If any meaning to these words could be proven through the help of an authentic dictionary, we will be grateful.

Rukhsaanah (رخشانه). No word as this appears in Arabic or Persian. But Rakhshaa(n) (رخشان) is a Persian word meaning illuminated, shining, glittering.

Zaareenah (زارينه). This word is perhaps derived from the Russian word Tzar (زار)–a title used for addressing a king in old Russia. Thus Zaareenah or Tzareenah (زارينه)–feminine of Zaar or Tzar–may have been formed by adding the Taa' of Ta'neeth according to the Arabic grammer.

Reshmaa(n) (ريشمان). This word is neither found in Arabic nor Persian. Perhaps it may be formed from the word Reesmaan (ريس مان) meaning thread, string in Persian.

Shaaheenah (شاهينه). Neither found in Arabic nor Persian. This word is formed–by adding the Taa' of Ta'neeth–from the Arabic word Shaaheen (شاهين). . . a royal falcon.

Naazalee (نازلى). This word is neither found in Arabic nor Persian. It is perhaps derived from the Arabic word Naazilah (نازلة) meaning calamity, accident, misfortune etc.. Muslims should abstain from names depicting calamities.

Roobeenah (روبينه). Perhaps this word is a derivation of the English word Ruby–a clear, deep-red variety of corundum, valued as a precious stone (Collins Concise English Dictionary). It is a common name amongst the Jewish rather than the English. Such names should not be kept by Muslims.

Tahmeenah (تهمينه). This name is neither found in Arabic nor Persian.

Aashee (عاشی). This name is neither found in Arabic nor Persian.

Afshaa (افشا). This word is neither found in Arabic nor Persian. But Ifshaa (افشا) is an Arabic word meaning to divulge a secret. There is a similar Persian word, Afshaa(n) (افشاں) which means confetti; strips of tinsel pasted on women's forehead as decoration.

Aneelah (انیله). Not found in Arabic nor Persian. But Aneelaa (انیلا) is an Urdu word meaning naive, inexperienced and mentally immature. In Gujrati there is a similar word, Aneel meaning wind.

Ruwaidah (رويده). This word is perhaps derived from the Arabic word Ruwaidan or Ruwaidaa (رويدا) meaning to give grace, to allow time, to defer, to postpone.

Farhaad (فرهاد). According to the authentic Persian dictionary "Loghaate-e-Kishvary", this is the name of a famous stone-cutter who was infatuated with a lady named Sheereen. Muslims should abstain from keeping such names.

NOTE: There are some names which are composed of two or more words. They are meaningless when in collective form, but have meaning when not. For example, Shamsul-Qamar, Roshan Aaraa and Zeenat Aaraa.
In Arabic there is a name Kulthoom. This name is usually given to girls whereas it is customary amongst Arabs to give this name to men. It would be more suitable as a female name when the word 'Um' is used as a prefix.

How to Find a Name

* NAMES IN THIS BOOK ARE LISTED IN STRICT ARABIC ALPHABETICAL ORDER AND ARE SET IN BOLDFACE TYPE.

* TO FIND A NAME ONE MUST BE ACQUAINTED WITH THE CORRECT ARABIC SPELLING OF THAT NAME SO THAT IT CAN BE SOUGHT FOR UNDER THE APPROPRIATE LETTER OF THE ARABIC ALPHABET. FOR INSTANCE, 'AADIL' WILL BE FOUND UNDER THE CHAPTER 'AIN' RATHER THAN 'ALIF'; 'SAALIHAH' WILL BE FOUND UNDER THE CHAPTER 'SAUD' RATHER THAN 'SEEN"; AND 'ZAAKIR" WILL BE FOUND UNDER THE CHAPTER 'ZAAL' RATHER THAN 'ZAA'.

* TO GIVE THE BEST PHONETIC RESULTS WE HAVE NOT SLAVISHLY ADHERED TO ITS GENERAL ENGLISH TRANSCRIPTION WHICH IS COMMONLY IN VOGUE. BUT WE CAN ASSURE YOU THAT THE TRANSCRIPTION LISTED IN THIS BOOK IS A HUMBLE EFFORT TOWARDS MAKING THE NAME SOUND, AS FAR AS POSSIBLE, LIKE ITS ARABIC VERSION--THOUGH NO GUARANTEE OF ACCURACY CAN BE GIVEN. HOWEVER, IT WOULD BE WISE IF AN AALIM IS CONSULTED FOR BEST RESULTS.

الف
The Chapter Alif

NAMES FOR BOYS

Aadam آدم
Name of the first man and prophet of Allah; father of mankind. The word Aadam is derived from the Arabic word *udmah* meaning wheat-coloured. Aadam *alayhis-salaam* was of this colour. Hence the name.

Aasif آصِف
Name of a courtier in the kingdom of Sulaimaan *alayhis-salaam* who was noted for his intelligence.
This name is commonly used in combination with Ali and Ahmad, as Asif Ali/Ahmad.

Abraar أَبْرَار
Plural of *barr*, meaning pious people; truthful persons; saints.
Suitable combination: Abraarul-Haqq.

Ibraaheem إِبْرَاهِيْم
Name of an illustrious prophet of Allah who was honoured with the title of *Khaleelullah* meaning friend of Allah. Ibraaheem literally means 'father of the people' or 'most affectionate father'.

Aboo أَبُوْ
Aboo literally means father. It forms a name or appellation when used in combination with names like Hasan, Haarith, Fadhl, Qaasim etc., except that *Alif Laam* will have to be inserted before the second portion of the name so as to join the preceding word with it, as Abul-Hasan, Abul-Haarith, Abul-Fadhl and Abul-Qaasim.

Elaboration: Abul-Haarith is another name for a lion. Abul-Fadhl is the appellation of Abbaas (RA). Abul-Qaasim is the appellation of Rasoolullah *sallallaahu-alayhi-wasallam*, meaning father of Qaasim since he had a son named Qaasim who passed away in his infancy.

Aboo Ayyoob أَبُوْ أَيّوب
A well-known Sahaabi who had received the honour of offering hospitality to Rasoolullah *sallallaahu-alayhi-wasallam* when he

migrated to Madinah.

Aboo Bakr أَبُوْ بَكر

Name of the first Khalifah of Islam, and the first amongst men to embrace Islam. A young camel is called *bakr* in Arabic. Aboo Bakr was known by this name since he was noted for his expertise in curing camels. His real name was Abdullah.

Aboo Toraab أَبُوْ تُرَاب

The appellation of Ali (RA). It was attributed to him by Rasoolullah *sallallaahu-alayhi-wasallam* when he found him one day lying flat on the bare floor of Masjidun-Nabi with dust on his body. Rasoolullah *sallallaahu-alayhi-wasallam* said to him humorously: *'Qum, Yaa Abaa Toraab!'–'Rise, O Father of Dust!'* This became his title ever since.

Aboo Haneefah ابُوْ حَنِيْفَة

The appellation of one of the four illustrious Imaams of the *Ahlus-sunnah-wal-jamaa'ah* whose real name was No'maan. The Imaam's extreme piety is borne out by the fact that for 43 years he performed all his daily *salaah* including *tahajjud* with one single *wudhu*. It was his custom to complete the recitation of the Holy Qur'aan 61 times during the holy month of Ramadaan.

Aboo Taalib ابُوْ طَالِب

The name of Rasoolullah's *sallallaahu-alayhi-wasallam* uncle and father of Ali (RA).

Aboo Ubaidah أَبُوْ عُبَيْدَة

Name of one of the ten sahaabah (RA) who, during their life time were given the glad tidings of their pardon and assured abode in Jannah.

Aboo Hurairah ابُوْ هُرَيْرَة

Name of an illustrious sahaabi (RA) who was noted for narrating and compiling thousands of Ahadeeth of Rasoolullah *sallallaahu-alayhi-wasallam.*

Ajmal اجْمَل

Extremely beautiful; handsome.

Ihtishaam إِحْتِشَام

Magnificence; pomp; glory.

Names usually kept are Ihtishaamul-Haqq, Ihtishaamul-Hasan.

Ahad احَد

One; unique; without partner; one of Allah's attributes.

Name: Abdul-Ahad.

Ihsaan إِحْسَان

Benevolent actions; favour; kindness.

Ideal combinations: Ihsaanullah, Ihsaanud-Deen, Ihsaanul-Haqq.

Ahmad أَحْمَد

The praised one; one worthy of praise; one who praises Allah abundantly; the blessed name of Rasoolullah *sallallaahu-alayhi-wasallam*. Suitable combinations are: Ahmadullah and Ahmadur-Rahmaan.

Ikhlaas إِخْلَاص

Sincerity; purity; selfless friendship.

Name: Ikhlaas Ahmad.

Akhlaaq اخْلَاق

Morals; virtue; good qualities; good manners; ethics.

Names: Akhlaaq Ahmad, Akhlaaq Husain.

Idrees إِدْرِيس

Name of an illustrious prophet of Allah. It is said that this word is derived from *dars* or *diraasah* meaning to read or teach the lesson. Owing to Idrees' (AS) reading and teaching the Holy Scriptures, he was called by this name.

Adeeb أَدِيب

A writer; author; one who inculcates ethical behaviour; intelligent.

Good combinations are Adeeb Ahmad and Adeebud-Deen.

Irshaad إِرْشَاد

To guide on the right path; to enjoin what is good; to instruct.

Names: Irshaad Ahmad and Irshaad Husain.

Arshad أَرْشَد

Most upright and honest; a well-guided person; most obedient.

Arshaq أَرْشَق

Handsome; one with a befitting height and a well-proportioned body.

Names normally kept are Arshaq Ali and Arshaq Ahmad.

Areeb أَرِيب

Wise; intelligent; expert.

A suitable combination is Areebud-Deen.

Azhar أَزْهَر

White; glittering; blooming; a face full of light.

Usaamah أُسَامَة

Name of a well-known sahaabi (RA).

Is'haaq إِسْحَاق

Name of a prophet of Allah and the son of Ibraaheem (AS). It means one who laughs. (Loghaatul-Qur'aan)

Asad اسد

Lion. Asadullah was the title of Sayyidona Ali *radhiyallahu-anhu*, meaning 'Lion of Allah'.

Israa'eel إسْرَائِيل

Another name of Siyyidona Ya'qoob (AS). Because of this name the Jews are referred to as Bani Israa'eel, meaning 'sons of Israa'eel'.

As'ad أسْعَد

Virtuous; pious; well-mannered; most fortunate.

Iskandar إسْكَنْدر

Name of a Greek king. Iskandar and Sikandar are both one and the the same.

Islaam إسْلَام

Literally it means to bow ones head in submission. Islamically it means submission to the will of Allah Ta'aalaa. The religion of the Muslims is called Islaam.

Suitable combination of names are ıslaamud-Deen, Islaam Ahmad.

Aslam أَسْلَم

Very safe; safeguarded; one who is protected from calamities and misfortunes. It is also the name of a sahaabi (RA).

Ismaa'eel إسْمَاعِيل

Name of a distinquished prophet of Allah, the son of Ibraaheem (AS). It is said that this name is composed of two words, *isma'* meaning *listen!* and *eel* meaning *Allah* in the Syriac language. In other words "Hear and grant my prayers, O Allah!" Ibraaheem (AS) used to make dua for a son by these words. When his dua was heard, he named the son *Ismaa'eel*. Ismaa'eel also means one who is obedient to Allah.

Usaid أُسَيْد

Diminutive form of *asad* meaning small lion.

Ishtiyaaq إشْتِيَاق

Yearning desire; fondness; eagerness.

Names: Ishtiyaaq Ahmad, Ishtiyaaq Husain.

Ashraf اشْرَف

Most noble; most distinguished; most eminent; of noble birth; a cultured person.

An ideal combination is Ashraf Ali.

Ashfaaq أَشْفَاق

Favours; kindness.

Istifaa' اِصْطِفاء

To choose; to prefer; to give preference to one over the other. Names: Istifaa' Ahmad, Istifaa' Husain.

Asgar اَصْغر

Smallest; minute.

Names: Asgar Ali and Asgar Husain.

Athar أَطْهَر

Most pious; meticulously neat and clean; chaste.

Atyab اطْيَبْ

Scrupulously clean; refined; most noble; excellent.

Azhar اظْهَر

Evident; most apparent; most illuminated.

Suitable combination of names: Azhar Ali and Azhar Husain.

I'jaaz إِعْجَاز

Miracle; *karaamah*; an event out of the usual course of nature.

A'dil أعْدِل

Having the highest calibre of justice.

I'zaaz اِعْزَاز

To respect and honour; to raise to an exalted position; to strengthen.

Names usually kept are I'zaaz Ali, I'zaaz Ahmad, I'zaaz Husain.

A'zam أَعْظَمْ

Most great; most pious; most exalted.

Note: Many people are in the habit of pronouncing this name as *A'jam* instead of *A'zam*. This is no ordinary mistake since *A'jam* means a mute.

Iftikhaar اِفْتِخَار

Honour; grace; glory; distinction; repute.

Afdhaal اَفْضَال

Plural of *fadl*. Kindness; grace; favours; virtue.

Afdhal افْضَل

Most excellent; prominent; most venerable.

Iqbaal إِقْبَال

Prosperity; good fortune; luck; success; felicity; blessings.

Akbar اَكْبَر

The greatest; most pious; honourable.

A good combination is Akbar Ali.

Ikraam اِكْرَام

Honouring; veneration; to pay respect.

Name: Ikraamud-Deen.

Akram أَكْرَم

Most gracious; benevolent; bountiful; most kind.

Altaaf أَلْطَاف

Plural of *lutf* meaning kindness; grace; favour; gift.

Suitable combinations are Altaaf Husain, Altaaf Ahmad.

Ulfat أُلْفَت

Friendship; intimacy; love; attachment; affection.

Ilyaas إِلْيَاس

Name of a prophet of Allah. He was called Ilyaaseen as well.

Imaam إِمَام

Leader; guide; The Qur'aan; The Caliph.

A suitable combination is Imaamud-Deen.

Amaan أَمَان

Safety; security; protection.

Name: Amaanullah.

Imtiyaaz إِمْتِيَاز

Distinction; to distinguish; wisdom; intelligent; sense.

Amjad أَمْجَد

Most glorious; most noble; most venerable; one with grandeur.

Imdaad إِمْدَاد

To assist; to support; the spreading of light during the day.

Suitable names: Imdaadullah, Imdaad Husain.

Ameer أَمِير

Commander; chieftain; ruler; a nobleman; a wealthy person.

Names: Ameer Ali, Ameerud-Deen.

Ameen أَمِين

Trustworthy; faithful; honest; trustee. Also the title of our beloved prophet, Muhammad *sallallaahu-alayhi-wasallam*. Prior to prophet-hood he was known to the Meccans as *Ameen* because of his honesty and nobility.

Anjum أَنْجُم

Plural of *najm*. Stars.

Anas أَنَس

Man; friend; one with whom bonds of intimacy exist. Name of an illustrious companion of Rasoolullah *sallallaahu-alayhi-wasallam*.

In'aam إِنْعَام

To confer favour; to present a gift; prize; reward.

Common names: In'aamullah, In'aamul-Haqq, In'aamul-Hasan

Anwaar أنوار
Plural of *noor* meaning light; lustre; brilliance.
Names: Anwaarul-Haqq, Anwaarul-Hasan.

Anwar أنور
Most bright; most brilliant; most beautiful.

Anees أنيس
One who makes acquaintances; friend; companion.

Uwais أويس
Name of a well-known saint who lived during the time of Rasoolullah *sallallaahu-alayhi-wasallam* and who, despite not having seen or met Rasoolullah *sallallaahu-alayhi-wasallam* admired and loved him whole-heartedly.

Ayyoob ايّوب
Name of a prophet of Allah known for forebearing hardships and difficulties with patient endurance.

NAMES FOR GIRLS

Aasiyah آسية
A mansion with solid foundation or pillars; a queen with a powerful dynasty: name of Fir'own's wife who had been executed by Fir'own after he discovered her Imaan.

Aaminah آمنة
A lady of peace and harmony. Name of the beloved mother of Rasoolullah *sallallaahu-alayhi-wasallam*.

Aanisah آنسة
A pious-hearted lady; good-natured; compatible.

Asmaa' اسماء
Plural of *ism* meaning names. Name of the beloved daughter of Aboo Bakr (RA).

Umme-Ayman امّ ايمن
Name of the lady who had breast-fed Rasoolullah *sallallaahu-alayhi-wasallam* whom The Prophet *sallallaahu-alayhi-wasallam* used to address as 'mother'.

Umme-Habeebah امّ حبيبة
Name of the sacred wife of Rasoolullah *sallallaahu-alayhi-wasallam.*

Umme-Roomaan امّ رومان
Name of the sacred wife of Sayyidona Aboo Bakr (RA) Hadhrat Aa'i'shah's (RA) beloved mother.

Umme-Salmah اُمِّ سَلَمَة

Name of one of the honourable wives of Rasoolullah *sallallaahu-alayhi-wasallam.*

Umme-Salmaa اُمِّ سَلْمٰى

Name of the beloved mother of Sayyidona Aboo Bakr (RA).

Umme-Kulthoom أُمِّ كُلْثُوْم

Name of the beloved daughter of Rasoolullah *sallallaahu-alayhi-wasallam.*

Umme-Haanee أُمِّ هَانِى

Name of the daughter of Aboo Taalib and sister of Ali (RA).

Amatullah أَمَةُ الله

Servant of Allah; name of a sahaabi (RA).

Ameenah أَمِيْنَة

Trustworthy; faithful; honest.

Anjum أَنْجُم

Plural of *najm*. Stars.

Aneesah أَنِيْسَة

Companion; an affectionate friend; name of a sahaabi (RA).

ب

The Chapter Baa

NAMES FOR BOYS

Baaizeed بَايُزِيْد
Name of a *walee* (saint) of Allah who lived in Bustaan.

Baaree بَارِیْ
Deity; creator; one of the attributes of the Almighty Allah.
Note: When a child is given a name where one of the attributes of Allah is desired to be used it is necessary that the word *Abd* meaning servant or slave be used as a prefix, as Abdul-Baaree meaning the slave or servant of the Creator or Deity.

Baasit بَاسِط
Conferer of prosperity; one of the attributes of Allah.
Name: Abdul-Baasit.

Baaqir بَاقِر
Fierce lion; deeply learned; a very wealthy man; the title of Imaam Aboo-Ja'far (RA).

Baaqee بَاقِی
The Everlasting; perpetual; an epithet of Allah.
Name: Abdul-Baaqee.

Badr بَدْر
The full moon of the fourteenth night of the lunar month; also name of a sahaabi (RA).
Suitable combinations are Badrud-Deen and Badre-Aalam.

Badee' بَدِيْع
Novel; strange; rare; wonderful; an attribute of Allah Ta'aalaa since Allah is the creator of things the like of which was hitherto non-existent.
Names: Badee'uz-Zamaan, Badee'ul-Laah.

Burhaan بُرْهَان
Proof; evidence.
Names: Burhaanud-Deen, Burhaanul-Laah, Burhaan Ahmad.

Bashaarat بَشَارَت
Good news; glad tidings.

Names commonly used are Bashaarat Ali and Bashaarat Ahmad.

Basheer بَشِيْر

One who gives glad tidings; an attribute of Rasoolullah *sallallaahu-alayhi-wasallam*.

Suitable combination of names: Basheer Ahmad, Basheerud-Deen.

Baseer بَصِيْر

Wise; sagacious; Allah's epithet.

Name: Abdul-Baseer.

Bilaal بِلاَل

Water; moisture; freshness; river; sea; ocean; name of the devoted Abyssinian *mu'azzin* of Rasoolullah *sallallaahu-alayhi-wasallam.*

Baleegh بَلِيْغ

Eloquent; learned; one who is qualified in the art of speech.

Name which is commonly given is Baleeghud-Deen.

Binyaameen بِنْيَامِيْن

Name of the brother of Yoosuf (AS).

Bahaa' بَهَاء

Beauty; elegance; excellence. It also means value in Persian.

Names: Bahaa'ud-Deen, Bahaa'ul-Laah.

NAMES FOR GIRLS

Batool بَتُوْل

Virgin; pure and chaste; a lady who is purely devoted to Allah; the title of Fatimah *radhiyallaahu-anhaa.*

Badr بَدْر

The full moon of the fourteenth night of the lunar month.

Name: Badrun-Nisaa'.

Bushraa بُشْرى

Glad tidings; good news.

Basheerah بَشِيْرَة

One who gives glad tidings; also the name of a sahaabi (RA).

Bilqees بِلْقِيْس

Name of the queen of Sabaa during the days of Sulaimaan (AS).

ت

The Chapter Taa

NAMES FOR BOYS

Taaj تاج
Crown.
Name: Taajud-Deen.

Tajammul تجمّل
To adorn or beautify oneself or to be adorned.
Names: Tajammul Ahmad/Husain.

Tasadduq تصدّق
To give *sadqah* or alms; to sacrifice; to strew generously.
Suitable names: Tasadduq Ali/Husain.

Taqee تقی
One who fears Allah; pious; devout.
Names: Taqee'ud-Deen, Muhammad Taqee, Taqee Ahmad/Husain.

Tamkeen تمکین
Majesty; Dignity; authority; power.

Tameez تمیز
Discernment; discretion; judgement; sense; distinction.
Names: Tameezud-Deen, Tameez Ahmad.

Tameem تمیم
Strong; one who has reached his full height; name of a sahabi (R.A.).

Tanweer تنویر
To illuminate; the appearance of light in the morning; the ripening of crops; the blooming of trees.
Names: Tanweer Ahmad/Husain/Ali, Tanweerud-Deen.

Tawfeeq توفیق
Divine guidance; the granting of a favourable situation by Allah.
Names: Tawfeeq Ahmad/Husain.

Tawqeer توقیر
Honour; respect; reverence; veneration.

Tahaw-wur تهوّر
Bravery; boldness; to plunge into some task without reluctance.

NAMES FOR GIRLS

Taa'ibah تَائِبَة

One who refrains from evil-doings; repentant.

Tabassum تَبَسُّم

Smile; a silent laugh where the lips do not part.

Tasneem تَسْنِيْم

Name of a fountain in Jannah; to elevate.

Tanweer *(see meaning on page 25)*

This name is used for boys as well as girls. For boys suffixes such as Ahmad, Ali etc. are used. For girls the word Tanweer is used by itself or with the word 'Baanoo' as suffix as is customary amongst the Indian Muslims of Uttar Pardesh.

ث

The Chapter Thaa

NAMES FOR BOYS

Thaabit ثَابِت
One who is well-established; brave; also the name of a well-known sahaabi (RA).

Thaaqib ثَاقِب
Shining brightly; glistening; splendid.
Names: Thaaqib Husain and Thaaqib Ahmad.

Tharwat ثَرْوَت
Wealth; power; influence.
This name is applicable to boys as well

Thanaa' ثَنَاء
Praise; applause; eulogy; glorification.
Name commonly used is Thanaa'ul-Laah.

NAMES FOR GIRLS

Tharwat *(see above)*

Thurai-yaa ثُرَيَّا
Clustre of seven brilliant stars in Taurus, commonly known as the 'seven sisters'; a wealthy lady; lustre; chandelier.

Thameenah ثَمِينَة
Costly; valuable; precious; excellent; exquisite.

ج

The Chapter Jeem

NAMES FOR BOYS

Jaabir جَابِر
Comforter; one who consoles the agrieved; name of a sahaabi (RA).

Jabbaar جَبَّار
Mighty; one who has the ascendency; king; one who commiserates the berieved; an attribute of Allah—hence the necessity of the word *Abd* before *Jabbaar* as Abdul-Jabbaar.

Ja'far جَعْفَر
River; riverlet; brook; canal; name of the cousin of the Prophet *sallallaahu-alayhi-wasallam* and blood brother of Ali (RA). After his demise Rasoolullah *sallallaahu-alayhi-wasallam* informed the sahaabah (RA) that Allah Ta'aalaa blessed him with wings in Jannah with which he goes wherever he pleases. Hence the title *Tayyaar*.

Jalaal جَلاَل
Grandeur; greatness; eminence; glory; majesty.
Suitable combinations: Jalaalud-Deen and Jalaal Ahmad.

Jaleel جَلِيْل
Great; glorious; illustrious; dignified; an attribute of Allah.
Suitable combinations: Jaleelur-Rahmaan and Abdul-Jaleel.

Jamaal جَمَال
Beauty; elegance; comeliness; of good looks and character.
Names: Mohammad Jamaal, Jamaalud-Deen, Jamaal Ahmad/Husain.

Jummal جُمَّل
A thick rope; a rope with which a boat is tied to the shore.

Jameel جَمِيْل
Handsome; physically and morally attractive; name of a sahaabi (RA).
A common name is Jameelur-Rahmaan.

Junaid جُنَيْد
A small army; name of a great saint who lived in Baghdaad.

Jawaad جَوَاد
Liberal; beneficient; bountiful; generous.
Names: Jawaad Ali, Jawaad Husain, Ali Jawaad, Ahmad Jawaad.

Jaw-waad جَوَّاد
Most beneficient; most bountiful; most generous.
Jauhar جَوْهَر
Diamond; gem; jewel; pearl; the essence of anything.
Jiyaad جِيَاد
Good; excellent; new; pure; speedy and swift.

NAMES FOR GIRLS

Jameelah جَمِيْلَة
A beautiful and elegant lady.
Juwairiyyah جُوَيْرِيَّة
Name of a sacred wife of Rasoolullah *sallallaahu-alayhi-wasallam.*

ح

The Chapter Haa

NAMES FOR BOYS

Haaris حَارِث
Ploughman; planter.

Haafiz حَافِظ
Guardian; preserver; one who commits the entire Qur'aan to memory.

Haamid حَامِد
One who praises and glorifies Allah; an attribute of Rasoolullah *sallallaahu-alayhi-wasallam*; also the name of a Sahabi (RA).
A common name: Haamidullah.

Habeeb حَبِيْب
Beloved; friend; Rasoolullah's *sallallaahu-alayhi-wasallam* attribute; name of a sahaabi (RA).
Combinations: Habeebur-Rahmaan, Habeebullah, Habeeb Ahmad.

Hosaam حُسَام
Sword.
A good combination: Hosaamud-Deen.

Hassaan حَسّان
Very pious; most wonderful; wise; name of a sahaabi (RA).

Husn حُسْن
Beauty; elegance; comeliness.
A suitable combination: Husnud-Deen.

Hasan حَسَن
Pious; good; fine; excellent; name of the beloved grandson of Rasoolullah *sallallaahu-alayhi-wasallam* ie. elder of the two sons of Ali and Fatimah *radhiyallaahu-anhumaa*.
An attractive combination: Hasanur-Rahmaan.

Haseeb حَسِيْب
A person with a noble lineage or family background; a reckoner.

Husain حُسَيْن
Diminutive form of *Hasan*. Pious; beautiful; handsome; name of the younger of the two sons of Ali (RA) and Faatimah (RA).

Hafs حَفْص
The offspring of a lion; also name of an Imaam of *qiraa'at*.

Hifz حِفْظ
To memorize; to preserve.
Name: Hifzur-Rahmaan.

Hafeez حَفِيْظ
Guardian; protector; an epithet applied to Allaho Ta'aalaa.
Names: Hafeezur-Rahmaan, Hafeezud-Deen, Abdul-Hafeez.

Haqq حَق
True; truth; right; Islaam; an attribute of Allah meaning 'The Truth'.
Names: Mobeenul-Haqq, Abdul-Haqq.

Hakam حَكَم
Mediate; arbitrator; an epithet applied to Allah.
Name: Abdul-Hakam.

Hakeem حَكِيْم
A sage; a philosopher; a physician; a wise person; Allah's attribute.
Names: Hakeemud-Deen and Abdul-Hakeem.

Haleem حَلِيْم
A patient man; one who perseveres; an attribute of Allaho Ta'aalaa.
Names: Abdul-Haleem, Haleemud-Deen, Mohammad Haleem.

Hammaad حَمَّاد
One who praises Allah without reservation; name of a sahaabi (RA).

Himaayat حِمَايَت
Protection; guardianship; patronage; support; defence.
Name: Himaayatul-Laah.

Hamdaan حَمْدَان
One who praises (Allah) excessively.

Hamzah حَمْزَة
Lion; name of the beloved uncle of Rasoolullah *sallallaahu-alayhi-wasallam* whose appellation was *Asadullaah* and *Asadur-Rasool* meaning 'Lion of Allah' and ' Lion of the Prophet'.

Hamood حَمُوْد
One who constantly glorifies and praises Allah; one who is much praised; one who is worthy of praise.
Name: Hamoodur-Rahmaan.

Hameed حَمِيْد *(same as Hamood)*
Name: Abdul-Hameed, Hameedullaah.

Humaid حُمَيْد
Diminutive of Hameed. Meaning is same as Hamood or Hameed.

Hannaan حَنَّان
Allah's attribute meaning Most Merciful and Most Forgiving. Name: Abdul-Hannaan.

Haneef حَنِيف
One who casts aside falsehood and professes the truth; one who abandons all false religions and follows Islaam steadfastly. The title of Ibraaheem (AS) attributed to him by Allah for his complete rejection of falsehood and resolute faith in the oneness of Allah.

Haidar حَيْدَر
A lion that mauls its prey to pieces; title of Ali *radhiyallahu-anhu*.

Hayy حَيّ
Ever-alive; an attribute applied exclusively to Allah. Name: Abdul-Hayy.

NAMES FOR GIRLS

Haarithah حَارِثَة
A (lady) farmer or cultivator; lioness.

Haarisah حَارِسَة
Guard; protector.

Haafizah حَافِظَة
Guardian; protector; a lady who has memorized the entire Qur'aan.

Haamidah حَامِدَة
One who praises and glorifies Allah; name of a lady sahaabi (RA).

Habeebah حَبِيْبَة
Beloved; another name for the holy city of Madinah Munaw-warah.

Hassaanah حَسَّانَة
Most pious; most beautiful; name of a lady sahaabi (RA).

Hasnaa' حَسْنَاء
A pious lady; a beautiful lady.

Husnaa حُسْنَى
Most pious; most beautiful; most precious.

Haseenah حَسِيْنَة
A beautiful lady; a girl with an attractive face.

Hafsah حَفْصَة
Name of the sacred wife of our beloved Rasool *alayhis-salaam* and the daughter of Umar *radhiyallaahu-anhu*.

Hafeezah حَفِيْظَة
Guardian; protector.

Haleemah حَلِيْمَة
A lady with a tenacity to patience and perseverence; name of the lady who had breast-fed Rasoolullah *sallallaahu-alayhi-wasallam.*

Hameedah حَمِيْدَة
One who praises Allah; the praised one; one worthy of praise.

Humairaa' حُمَيْرَاء
A beautiful girl with a ruddy complexion; white; Aa'ishah's (RA) title

Haneefah حَنِيْفَة
One who rejects falsehood and follows the truth.

Haw-waa حَوّا
A beautiful girl with a ruddy complexion and somewhat dark lips; name of the wife of Aadam *alayhis-salaam*—mother of mankind.

خ

The Chapter Khaa

NAMES FOR BOYS

Khaalid خَالِد

Permanent; durable; one who does not grow weak even in old age; name of a well-known and brave sahaabi, Khaalid bin Waleed (RA).

Khaaliq خَالِق

The Creator; one who creates things from non-existence.
Name: Abdul-Khaaliq.

Khabeer خَبِيْر

Informer; Allah's epithet meaning knower of everything.
Name: Abdul-Khabeer.

Khateeb خَطِيْب

An orator; one who delivers the *khutbah* on Jumu'ah and other auspicious occasions.

Khaleeq خَلِيْق

Of good disposition; kind; benign; well-disposed.
Names: Mohammad Khaleeq, Khaleequz-Zamaan.

Khaleel خَلِيْل

A sincere friend; *Khaleelullah* was the title of Sayyidona Ibraaheem (AS) meaning 'friend of Allah'.
Names: Khaleelullah, Khaleelur-Rahmaan, Khaleel Ahmad.

NAMES FOR GIRLS

Khaalidah خَالِدَة

Permanent; long-living; one who does not grow weak even after attaining old age; name of a sahaabi (RA).

Khadeejah خَدِيْجَة

Name of the beloved wife of Rasoolullah *sallallaahu-alayhi-wasallam.*

Khawlah خَوْلَة

A buck; deer; name of a well-known sahaabi (RA).

Khairun-Nisaa' خَيْرُ النِّسَاء

The best amongst ladies; the most beautiful amongst ladies.

د

The Chapter Daal

NAMES FOR BOYS

Daanyaal دَانيَال
Name of a prophet of Allah Ta'aalaa.

Daawood دَاوٗود
A prophet to whom the *Zaboor* was revealed; father of Sulaimaan *alayhis-salaam.*

Daulah دَوْلَة
Riches; happiness; felicity; prosperity.
Names: Aasifud-Daulah, Daulat Ali.

Deen دِيْن
Faith; religion.
Names: Saleemud-Deen, Ikraamud-Deen, Fakhrud-Deen.

Daiyaan دَيّان
A mighty ruler; judge; guard; potector; one who does not render any deed worthless but compensates accordingly; Allah's attribute.
Name: Abdud-Dayyaan.

NAMES FOR GIRLS

Durrah دُرَّة
A large or precious pearl; name of a sahaabi (RA).

ذ

The Chapter Zaal*

NAMES FOR BOYS

Zaakir ذاكِر
One who constantly praises and remembers Allaho Ta'aalaa.
Names: Zaakir Husain, Zaakir Ahmad, Zaakir Hasan.

Zakaa' ذَكاء
Keen perception; sharpness of mind; deep insight; sagacity.
Name: Zakaa'ud-Deen.

Zokaa' ذُكاء
The sun; dawn; morning.
Names: Zokaa'ur-Rahmaan, Zokaa'ul-Laah, Zokaa'ud-Deen.

Zakee ذَكِيّ
One who has a sharp mind and keen perception; intelligent.
Name: Zakiyyud-Deen.

Zulfaqaar ذُو الْفَقار
Name of a celebrated sword which fell into the hand of Rasoolullah *sallallaahu-alayhi-wasallam* in the Battle of Badr and which was then presented to Ali (RA). Note: It is incorrect to say *Fiqaar*—with *kasrah*.

Zul-Kifl ذُو الْكِفْل
Name of a prophet of Allah.

Zun-Noon ذُو النُّون
The appellation of Yoonus (AS) meaning The Man of the Whale, since he was swallowed by a whale; also name of a saint—Zun-Noon Misree.

NAMES FOR GIRLS

Zaakirah ذاكِرَة
One who constantly remembers and glorifies Allah.

Zaakiyah ذاكِيَة
A lady with keen perception and a sharp mind; an intelligent lady.

---

*Also transliterated as ḌAAL or THAAL.

Zakiyyah زَكِيَّة

A lady with a sharp mind and keen perception; intelligent.

ر - ل

The Chapter Raa

NAMES FOR BOYS

Raashid رَاشِد
Pious; follower of the right path.

Raaghib رَاغِب
Willing; desirous; inclined towards...anything.

Rabb رَبّ
The Sustainer; master; an attribute of Allah.
Name: Abdur–Rabb.

Rabbaanee رَبَّانِى
One who is attached to Allah; devotee; one possessing knowledge of Allah and His kingdom. The word 'Ghulaam' is usually used as a prefix as Ghulaam Rabbaanee.

Rahmaan رَحْمَان
Allah's attribute meaning Most Merciful, Most Kind.
Suitable combination of names are: Hasanur-Rahmaan, Jaleelur-Rahmaan, Azeezur-Rahmaan, Abdur-Rahmaan, Ahmadur-Rahmaan, Shafeequr-Rahmaan, Hifzur-Rahmaan, Hafeezur-Rahmaan, Khaleelur-Rahmaan, Ateequr-Rahmaan, Fadhlur-Rahmaan, Mahfoozur-Rahmaan.

Rahmat رَحْمَت
Sympathy; mercy.
Name: Rahmatul-Laah.

Raheem رَحِيْم
Allah's epithet meaning Most Merciful, Most Kind.
Name: Abdur-Raheem.

Razzaaq رَزَّاق
Allah's attribute meaning The Provider, The Sustainer.
Name: Abdur-Razzaaq.

Rasool رَسُوْل
Messenger; messenger of Allah.
Names: Abdur-Rasool, Ghulaam Rasool.

Rashaad رَشَاد
To acquire guidance; to lead a righteous life.
Rasheed رَشِيْد
Righteous; one who guides on the right path; Allah's attribute.
Names: Rasheed, Abdur-Rasheed.
Ridhaa رِضَا
Pleasure; contentment; approval.
Names: Ahmad Ridhaa, Ridhaa Ali.
Ridhwaan رِضْوَان
Pleasure; happiness; Jannah; doorkeeper of Jannah.
Radhee رَضِى
A lover; suitor.
Name: Riyaadhud-Deen.
Rif'at رِفْعَت
Dignity; exaltation; eminence; nobility.
Name: Mohammad Rif'at.
Rafee' رَفِيْع
High; sublime; exalted; of nobility and dignity.
Names: Mohammad Rafee', Rafee' Ahmad, Rafee'ud-Deen.
Rafeeq رَفِيْق
Friend; associate; companion; a soft- and kind-hearted person.
Ra'oof رَؤُوْف
An attribute applied to Allah, meaning Most Merciful, Most Kind. Rasoolullah *sallallaahu-alayhi-wasallam* is also referred to as *Ra'oof* in the Holy Qur'aan.
Name: Abdur-Ra'oof.
Ra'ees رَئِيْس
Leader; chief; captain; prince; nobleman.
Name: Ra'ees Ahmad.
Riyaadh رِيَاض
Gardens; Jannah.
Name: Riyaadhud-Deen.
Rayhaan رَيْحَان
A sweet-smelling plant; any flower besides rose; comfort.

NAMES FOR GIRLS

Raabi'ah رَابِعَة
Fourth; name of a saint who lived in Basrah.

Raashidah رَاشِدَة
Pious; righteous; follower of the right path.

Raadhiyah رَاضِيَة
Pleased; happy; contented.

Rabee'ah رَبِيْعَة
Abounding in green foliage.

Raheemah رَحِيْمَة
Kind; affectionate.

Rasheedah رَشِيْدَة
Righteous; of good character; one who leads onto the right path.

Ridhwaanah رِضْوَانَة
Pleasure; contentment.

Radhiyyah رَضِيَّة
Pleased; delighted; contented.

Ra'naa رَعْنَا
Lovely; beautiful; graceful; delicate.

Rif'at رِفْعَت
Dignity; exaltation; eminence; nobility.

Rafee'ah رَفِيْعَة
High; sublime; exalted; a lady of honour and nobility.

Rafeeqah رَفِيْقَة
Friend; associate; companion; a soft- and kind-hearted lady.

Ruqaiyah رُقَيَّة
Name of the beloved daughter of Rasoolullah *sallallaahu-alayhi-wasallam.*

Rumaanah رُمَانَة
A pomegranate seed.

Ra'eesah رَئِيْسَة
Leader; chief; princess; a noble lady; a wealthy lady.

Raihaanah رَيْحَانَة
A bouquet of flowers; a sweet-smelling flower; name of a sahaabi.

ز - Z

The Chapter Zaa

NAMES FOR BOYS

Zaahid زَاهِد
A devotee; an ascetic; one who renounces the world and is fully devoted to Allah.
Names: Zaahid Husain, Zaahid Ahmad.

Zaahir زَاهِر
A blooming flower; a bright and shining colour; lofty.

Zubaid زُبَيْد
The diminutive of *zubd* meaning cream, butter etc.

Zubair زُبَيْر
A brave and wise person; name of one of the *Asharah Mubash-shrah.**

Zufar زُفَر
Lion; a brave person; an army; a flowing river; name of an authority in *fiqh* during the time of Imaam Aboo Haneefah (RA).

Zakariyyaa زَكَرِيَّا
Name of a prophet of Allah.

Zakee زَكِيّ
Pure; virtuous; clean; truthful.
Names: Zakee Ahmad, Zakiyyud-Deen.

Zaheer زَهِيْر
Blooming; shining; luminous.

Ziyaad زِيَاد
Increase; surplus; plenty.

Zaid زَيْد
Abundance; excess; surplus; name of a sahaabi *radhiyallaahu-anhu.*

Zain زَيْن
Ornament; beauty; grace; honour; to beautify; to decorate.
Suitable combination of names: Zainul-Aabideen, Zainud-Deen.

---

*The ten Sahabahs who were given the glad tidings of their assured attainment of Jannah by Rasoolullah (sallallaahu-alayhi-wasallam).

NAMES FOR GIRLS

Zaahidah زَاهِدَة
A hermit; a lady who renounces this world and devotes herself fully to Allah.

Zaahirah زَاهِرَة
A blooming flower; of bright and lovely colour; lofty.

Zubaidah زُبَيْدَة
Diminutive of *zubdah*. Cream; butter.

Zahraa' زَهْرَاء
Beautiful; also the name of The Lady of Jannah, Faatamah (RA).

Zuhrah زُهْرَة
The planet venus; beauty; virtue; elegance; splendour.

Zahrah زَهْرَة
Spirit; courage; power; freshness; flower.

Zakiyyah زَكِيَّة
Pure; virtuous; clean; truthful; affluent; fertile land.

Zulaikhah زُلَيْخَة
A lady with such beauty that it leaves people gaping in wonderment.

Zaleekhah زَلِيْخَة
Meaning is same as above.

Zaib زَيْب
Beauty.
Name: Zaibun-Nisaa'–the most beautiful amongst ladies.

Zaitoon زَيْتُوْن
The olive tree or the olive fruit.

Zaitoonah زَيْتُوْنَة
Singular of *zaitoon* meaning one olive.

Zainab زَيْنَب
Name of a beautiful tree exuding fragrance; name of the elder daughter of Rasoolullah *sallallaahu-alayhi-wasallam;* also name of one of his sacred wives.

Zeenat زِيْنَت
Beauty; elegance; adornment.
A suitable combination: Zeenatun-Nisaa'.

س

The Chapter Seen

NAMES FOR BOYS

Saajid سَاجِد
One who is in the position of prostrating *(making sajdah)*.
Name: Saajid Ali.

Saalim سَالِم
Safe; sound; perfect; complete.

Subbooh سُبُّوح
Extremely pure; Allah's attribute.
Name: Abdus-Subbooh.

Sattaar سَتَّار
An attribute of Allah meaning one who conceals faults...by the veil of His mercy.
Name: Abdus-Sattaar.

Sajjaad سَجَّاد
One who constantly prostrates *(makes sajdah)*.
Names: Sajjaad Ali, Sajjaad Husain; Sajjaad Ahmad.

Siraaj سِرَاج
Lamp; the sun; candle.
Names: Siraaj Ahmad, Siraajud-Deen.
Note: It is incorrect to pronounce this word as *Shiraaz*, for *Shiraaz* is the name of a town in Iran. The correct pronunciation is *Si-raaj*.

Sa'aadat سَعَادَت
Prosperity; happiness; good fortune; auspiciousness.
Name: Sa'aadat Husain.

Sa'd سَعْد
Felicity; prosperity; name of one of the *Ashar Mubash-sharah* ie. the 10 sahaabah (RA) who were given the good news of their pardon and assured abode in Jannah.
Names: Sa'dud-Deen and Sa'dullah.

Sa'ood سَعُوْد
Fortunate; pious; auspicious, prosperous.

Sa'eed سَعِيْد

Fortunate; auspicious; venerable; dignified; name of a sahaabi (RA).

Sufyaan سُفْيَان

Name of a well-known sahaabi (RA).

Sikandar *(see Iskandar page 18)*

Silaah سِلاح

Arms; armour; weapons.

Name: Silaahud-Deen.

Salaam سَلام

Salvation; peace; free from any blemish or vice; attribute of Allah.

Name: Abdus-Salaam.

Sultaan سُلْطَان

King; emperor; power; victory; conquest; proof.

Salmaan سَلْمَان

One who is safeguarded against all calamities; mild; affable; perfect; of cool temperament.

Saleem سَلِيْم

Mild; affable; perfect; healthy; guarded against calamities.

Sulaimaan سُلَيْمَان

Name of a prophet of Allah; blessed son of Daawood *alayhis-salaam*

Sameer سَمِيْر

One who narrates stories or tales in the night; a story-teller.

Samee' سَمِيْع

Allah's epithet meaning The Listener, The Knower.

Names: Abdus-Samee', Samee'ul-Haqq, Samee'ud-Deen.

Sahl سَهْل

Easy; soft; smooth; soft soil; contented.

Suhail سُهَيْل

The star Canopus.

Name: Suhail Ahmad.

Saif سَيْف

Sword; *Saifullah* was the title of Khaalid bin Waleed *radhiyallaahu-anhu* meaning 'Sword of Allah'.

Names: Saifud-Deen and Saifur-Rahmaan.

NAMES FOR GIRLS

Saajidah سَاجِدَة
Prostrating in prayer *(salaah)*; one who *makes sajdah.*

Saarah سَارَة
Name of the sacred wife of Ibraaheem (AS); mother of Is'haaq (AS) It means sheet or veil.

Saar-rah سَارَّة
A lady whose charming manner causes joy and happiness.

Saahirah سَاهِرَة
Earth; moon; a spring which flows constantly.

Sa'diyah سَعْدِيَة
Good fortune; happiness; blessed; name of the lady who had breast-fed Rasoolullah *sallallaahu-alayhi-wasallam*—Haleemah Sa'diyah.

Sa'eedah سَعِيْدَة
Fortunate; auspicious; august; venerable; name of a sahaabi (RA).

Sakeenah سَكِيْنَة
Comfort; ease; something by which comfort is acquired; rest.

Sukainah سُكَيْنَة
Diminutive of *sakeenah*. Meaning is same as above.

Salaamah سَلَامَة
Salvation; peace; free from blemish; ease; name of a sahaabi (RA).

Sultaanah سُلْطَانَة
Queen; ruler.

Salmah سَلْمَة
To obey; to bow the head in submission and obedience.

Salmaa سَلْمٰى
Name of an extremely beautiful Arab lady. Therefore, metaphorically, a beloved could be called *'Salmaa'*.

Saleemah سَلِيْمَة
Mild; affable; healthy; without defect; protected from calamities; having a calm and serene disposition; tolerant.

Sameerah سَمِيْرَة
One who narrates stories in the night; a story-teller.

Sameenah سَمِيْنَة
A healthy girl; fertile land without rock and stone.

Sumaiyah سُمَيَّة
Name of a lady sahaabi (RA) who was the first amongst ladies to be martyred for Islaam.

Saudah سَوْدَة
Name of one of the honourable wives of Rasoolullah *sallallaahu-alayhi-wasallam.*
Suhailah سُهَيْلَة
Canopy; tent; marquee.
Saiyidah سَيِّدَة
Lord; chief.

ش

The Chapter Sheen

NAMES FOR BOYS

Shaafee شَافِیْ
Healer; restorer of health; one of the attributes of Allaho Ta'aalaa.
Name: Abdush-Shaafee.

Shaakir شَاكِر
Grateful; contented.

Shaahid شَاهِد
Witness; angel; day of Jumu'ah; day of Qiyaamah; an attribute of Rasoolullah *sallallaahu-alayhi-wasallam.*

Shaaheen شَاهِيْن
A royal, white falcon.

Shabbeer شَبّیْر
Beautiful; virtuous; dignified; title of Imaam Husain *radhiyallaah-anh.*
Common name: Shabbeer Ahmad.

Shujaa' شُجَاع
Brave; bold.
Names: Shujaa'ud-Deen, Shujaa'ul-Laah, Shujaa'ur-Rahmaan.

Shujaa'at شُجَاعَت
Bravery; valour; fearlessness.
Name: Shujaa'at Ali.

Shajee' شَجِيْع
Brave; bold; fearless.

Sharf شَرَف
Honour; honour and esteem due to some meritorious achievement.
Name: Sharfud-Deen.

Shareef شَرِيْف
Noble; eminent; legitimate; chief of a tribe; one with an honourable family background; urbane.

Shu'aa' شُعَاع
The rays of the sun; sunshine; light; lustre; splendour.
Suitable combinations: Shu'aa'ur-Rahmaan, Shu'aa'ud-Deen.

Shuaib شُعَيْب
Name of an illustrious prophet of Allaho Ta'aalaa.

Shafaa'at شَفَاعَت
Intercession; recommendation; entreaty.
Names: Shafaa'at Ahmad, Shafaa'at Husain, Shafaa'at Ali.

Shafee' شَفِيْع
Intercessor; mediator; an attribute of Nabi *sallallaahu-alayhi-wasallam.*
Name: Mohammad Shafee'.

Shafeeq شَفِيْق
Affectionate; compassionate; a kind-hearted friend.
Names: Shafeeq Ahmad, Shafeequr-Rahmaan.

Shakoor شَكُوْر
Most grateful; one who gives due appreciation; one who can appreciate the worth of any deed; an attribute of Allaho Ta'aalaa.
Name: Abdush-Shakoor.

Shakeel شَكِيْل
Comely; handsome; well-shaped; well-formed.
Name: Shakeel Ahmad.

Shams شَمْس
The sun.
Names: Shamsud-Deen, Shamsul-Haqq.

Shameem شَمِيْم
Fragrant; scent; a sweet-smelling breeze; lofty.
Name: Shameemud-Deen.

Shaukat شَوْكَت
Dignity; magnificence; grandeur; pomp; power.
Name: Shaukat Ali.

Shahaab شَهَاب
Flame; brightness of flame; meteor; a man of experience.
Name: Shihaabud-Deen.

Shaheed شَهِيْد
Present; witness; one who gives evidence based on truth; a martyr.

Shaikh شَيْخ
Chief; an experienced man; an old man.

NAMES FOR GIRLS

Shaakirah شَاكِرَة
Grateful; contented.

Shaahidah شَاهِدَة
Witness; name of a sahaabi (RA).

Shajee'ah شَجِيْعَة
Brave; bold; courageous.

Sharfaa' شَرْفَاء
A most noble and honourable lady; name of a sahaabi (RA).

Shareefah شَرِيْفَة
Noble; eminent; legitimate; gentle; urbane.

Shafee'ah شَفِيْعَة
Intercessor; mediator.

Shafeeqah شَفِيْقَة
Affectionate; compassionate; a kind-hearted friend.

Shakeelah شَكِيْلَة
Comely; beautiful; well-formed; well-shaped.

Shamaamah شَمَامَة
The fragrance of scent or *itr;* perfume.

Shamoodah شَمُوْدَة
Diamond.

Shameelah شَمِيْلَة
Natural disposition; character; quality; virtue; a young shoot; a bud.

Shameemah شَمِيْمَة
Fragrant; sweet-smelling scent; a sweet breeze.

Shahlaa شَهْلا
Having grey eyes with a shade of red; a species of the Nacissus flower.

ص

The Chapter Saad*

NAMES FOR BOYS

Saabir صَابِر
One who patiently and stoically endures all hardships and difficulties; title of Ayyoob *alayhis-salaam*.

Saadiq صَادِق
True; sincere; faithful; veracious; a man of his word.

Saalih صَالِح
Virtuous; chaste; righteous; name of a well-known prophet of Allah.

Sabeeh صَبِيْح
Beautiful; handsome; one with a fair complexion.
Names with good combination: Sabeeh Ahmad, Sabeehud-Deen.

Saboor صَبُوْر
Patient; forebearing; one who overlooks the faults of others.
Name: Abdus-Saboor.

Sadr صَدْر
The breast; chest; bosom; the highest part; the highest person; chief.
Name: Sad-rud-Deen.

Siddeeq صِدِّيْق
Just; true; sincere; a sincere friend; one who is true in word and deed; title of Sayyidona Aboo Bakr *radhiyallaahu-anhu*.

Sagheer صَغِيْر
Small; slender; tender.
Names: Sagheer Ahmad, Sagheer Husain.

Safdar صَفْدَر
A violent warrior; one who breaks the enemy's ranks.
Names: Safdar Husain, Safdar Ali.

Safwaan صَفْوَان
Hard rock having lustre; a cold, cloudless day; name of a sahaabi.

***Sometimes transliterated as SAUD or SUAAD**

Safee صَفِى
Pure; just; righteous; pious; a sincere friend; title of Sayyidona Aadam *alayhis-salaam* was *Safiyyul-Laah* meaning *Allah's Friend.*

Salaah صَلاح
Peace; concord; treaty; rectitude or moral uprightness.
Name: Salaahud-Deen.

Samad صَمَد
The Eternal; High; one who is not dependent on anyone and on whom everyone and everything is dependent: Allah's attribute.
Name: Abdus-Samad.

Saulat صَوْلَت
Pomp; dignity; majesty.
Names: Saulat Husain, Saulat Ahmad.

NAMES FOR GIRLS

Saabirah صَابِرَة
One who endures hardships stoically and with great endurance.

Saadiqah صَادِقَة
True; sincere; faithful; veracious; a lady whose word is her honour.

Saalihah صَالِحَة
Virtuous; a chaste woman; righteous.

Sabeehah صَبِيْحَة
Beautiful; handsome; a lady with a fair complexion.

Sughraa صُغْرَى
Small; smallest; name of the younger daughter of Imaam Husain (RA)

Sagheerah صَغِيْرَة
Small; slender; tender.

Safiyyah صَفِيَّة
Pure; righteous; the most valuable portions of the spoils of battle; a palm tree bearing much fruit; name of one of the honourable wives of Rasoolullah *sallallaahu-alayhi-wasallam.*

ض

The Chapter Dhaad

NAMES FOR BOYS

Dhaamin ضَامِن
One who stands surety for another; one who helps.
Name: Dhaamin Ahmad.

Dhiyaa' ضِيَاء
Light; splendour; brilliance.
Names: Dhiyaa-ul-Haq, Dhiyaa-ud-Deen, Dhiyaa-ur-Rahmaan.

ط

The Chapter Tau

NAMES FOR BOYS

Taariq طَارِق
The morning star; a night-traveller; name of a great Muslim warrior who conquered Spain. *Jabal-al-Taariq* which has been changed to *Gibralter* is named after him. Also the name of a sahaabi (RA).

Taalib طَالِب
A seeker; an enquirer; a lover.
Names: Aboo Taalib, Taalibur-Rahmaan, Taalib Husain.

Taahaa طٰهٰ
Name of a *surah* in the Holy Qur'aan.
An ideal combination: Taahaa Husain.

Taahir طَاهِر
Pure; chaste; pious; clean; name of a sahaabi (RA).

Tufail طُفَيْل
Intercession; mediation; name of a sahaabi (RA).

Talhah طَلْحَة
Name of a sahaabi (RA).

Tal'at طَلْعَت
Appearance; countenance.
Name: Tal'at Husain.

Tay-yib طَيِّب
Good; sweet; agreeable; pure; chaste; *halaal.*

NAMES FOR GIRLS

Taahirah طَاهِرَة
Pure; chaste; pious; clean.

Taybah طَيْبَة
Pure; excellent; another name for the holy city of Madinah.

Tay-yibah طَيِّبَة
Good; sweet; agreeable; pure; chaste; *halaal*; blessed; an atttibute of Madinah.

ظ

The Chapter Zhau

NAMES FOR BOYS

Zaahir ظَاهِر
Apparent; evident; one of the attributes of Allah Ta'ala.
Name: Zaahir Husain.

Zafar ظَفَر
Victory; triumph; name of a sahaabi (RA).
Names: Zafar Husain, Zafar Ahmad.

Zafeer ظَفِيْر
Of firm and resolute intention.
Name: Zafeerud-Deen.

Zuhoor ظُهُوْر
Appearing; arising; visibility.
Names: Zuhoor Ahmad, Zuhoor Husain.

Zaheer ظَهِيْر
An ally; an associate; a protector.
Names: Zaheer Ahmad, Zaheerul-Islaam.

NAMES FOR GIRLS

Zaheerah ظَهِيْرَة
An ally; an associate; a protector.

ع

The Chapter Ain

NAMES FOR BOYS

Aabid عَابِد
Worshipper; devotee; devout.
Good combinations: Aabid Husain/Ali; Aabidullah.

Aatiq عَاتِق
Free; liberated; independent.
Name: Aatiq Ali.

Aadil عَادِل
Just; upright; sincere; attribute of Nabi *sallallaahu-alayhi-wasallam.*

Aarif عَارِف
One who possesses knowledge of Allah and His kingdom; a devotee.

Aashiq عَاشِق
A lover; a suitor.
Names: Aashiq Ali, Aashiq Ilaahee.

Aasim عَاصِم
Chaste; protected; safe; name of a great Imaam of *Tajweed.*

Aaqil عَاقِل
Wise; intelligent; sensible.

Aalam عَالَم
The world; the universe; *Aalamgheer* was the name of a king of the Mugal dynasty–*Aurangzeb.*
Name: Badr-e-Aalam.

Aamir عَامِر
One who inhabits; one who performs *umrah*; name of a sahaabi.

Ubaadah عُبَادَة
Name of a prominent sahaabi *radhiyallaahu-anhu.*

Abd عَبْد
A servant; a devotee; a slave. This word is used in combination with the word *Allah* or any attribute of Allah Ta'ala and His Rasool eg. Abdullah, Abdul-Haqq, Abdur-Rasool, Abdun-Nabi.

Abbaas عَبَّاس
A furious lion that mauls its prey to pieces; pomp; name of the

uncle of Rasoolullah *sallallaahu-alayhi-wasallam.*

Ubaid عُبَيْد

Diminutive of *Abd* meaning 'small servant'. Ubaidullah was the name of a sahaabi (RA) as well.

Names: Ubaidul-lah, Ubaidur-Rahmaan, Ubaidul-Haqq.

Ateeq عَتِيْق

Ancient; antiquated; liberated. Title of Sayyidona Aboo Bakr (RA).

Name: Ateequr-Rahmaan.

Uthmaan عُثْمَان

The young of a lark; a beautiful pen; name of the third Caliph of Islam.

Adnaan عَدْ نَان

Name of a leader of the tribe of Quraish. The Prophet *sallallaahu-alayhi-wasallam* was from this tribe.

Adeel عَدِ يْل

One who dispenses justice.

Irfaan عِرْفَان

Knowledge; discernment; science; wisdom; knowledge of Allah Ta'ala and His kingdom.

Urwah عُرْوَة

Name of a prominent sahaabi *radhiyallaahu-anhu.*

Uzair عُزَيْر

Name of a prophet of Allah Ta'ala.

Azeez عَزِيْز

Dear; beloved; respected; esteemed; precious; powerful; rare; an attribute of Allah Ta'ala.

Names: Azeezur-Rahmaan/-Deen, Azeez Ahmad, Abdul-Azeez.

Ataa' عَطَاء

A gift; present; favour; bounty; generosity.

Names: Ataa'ul-lah, Ataa'ur-Rahmaan, Ataa'ul-Haqq.

Azeem عَظِيْم

Great; dignified; exalted. An epithet of Allah Ta'ala.

Names: Abdul-Azeem, Azeemud-Deen.

Uqbah عُقْبَة

Name of an illustrious sahaabi *radhiyallaahu-anhu.*

Aqeel عَقِيْل

A wise, intelligent and sensible man; name of Ali's (RA) brother.

Ikramah عِكْرَمَة

A female pigeon; name of an illustrious sahaabi *radhiyallaahu-anhu.*

Alaa' عَلاَء

Name: Alaa'ud-Deen.

Glory; sublimity; superiority.

Alee (usually spelt Ali) عَلِى

Sublime; eminent; honourable; Allah's attribute; son-in-law and cousin of Rasoolullah *sallallaahu-alayhi-wasallam.*

Names: Ahmad Ali, Muhammad Ali, Zubair Ali, Abbaas Ali.

Aleem عَلِيْم

Wise; learned; omniscient; an epithet applied to Allah Ta'ala.

Names: Abdul Aleem, Aleemud-Deen.

Imaad عِمَاد

A pillar; a military envoy.

Names: Imdaadud-Deen, Imdaadul-Haqq.

Ammaar عَمّار

One with strong *imaan*; tolerant; of dignity; one who is punctual in *salaah* with *jamaa'ah*; name of a sahaabi (RA).

Umar عُمَر

Name of the second caliph of Islaam.

Amr عَمْرو

Name of a well-known sahaabi *radhiyallaahu-anhu.*

Imraan عِمْرَان

Population; civilization; careful observance of rules of etiquette; affibility. Name of the father of Maryam *alayhas-salaam.*

Inaayat عِنَايَت

Favour; bounty; kindness.

Names: Inaayat Ahmad; Inaayat Husain; Inaayatul-Lah.

Eesaa (usually spelt Isa) عِيْسٰى

Name of a well-known prophet of Allah. He is also known as *Maseeh* and *Roohul-Lah.*

NAMES FOR GIRLS

Aabidah عَابِدَة
Worshipper; devotee; devout.

Aatiqah عَاتِقَة
Emancipated; a beautiful lady; of honourable family background.

Aatikah عَاتِكَة
A lady who is richly perfumed.

Aadilah عَادِلَة
Just; upright; sincere; righteous.

Aarifah عَارِفَة
A lady possessing knowledge of Allah and His kingdom; a devotee.

Aasimah عَاصِمَة
Safe; chaste; virtuous; a title for the holy city of Madinah.

Aatirah عَاطِرَة
Of good fragrance; a connoisseur of fragrance.

Aaqilah عَاقِلَة
Wise; sensible; intelligent.

Aakifah عَاكِفَة
A lady who worships Allah in solitude.

Aamirah عَامِرَة
An occupant of an abode; one who makes *umrah* or *ziyaarah*; abundant treasure.

Aa'ishah (usually spelt Ayesha) عَائِشَة
A prosperous, happy and fortunate lady; name of the sacred wife of Rasoolullah *sallallaahu-alayhi-wasallam*; Aboo Bakr's (RA) daughter.

Azraa عَذْرَاء
A young lady; an unpierced pearl retaining its pristine beauty; the title attributed to Maryam (AS), the mother of Eesaa (AS).

Azeezah عَزِيْزَة
Dear; respected; esteemed; precious; rare; powerful.

Ismat عِصْمَت
Chastity; honour; protection.

Atiyyah عَطِيَّة
A grant; a gift; bounty; present.

Azeemah عَظِيْمَة
Great; encompassing; dignified.

Iffat عِفّت
Purity; chastity; modesty; virtue; abstinence.

Afraa' عَفْرَاء

A lady with a fair complexion; a buck.

Afeefah عَفِيْفَة

Pure; chaste; modest; decent; upright.

Aqeelah عَقِيْلَة

A wise and intelligent lady; a sensible lady; name of a lady sahaabi.

Ammaarah عَمَّارَة

A lady with strong *imaan*; tolerant; a lady who is most punctual in carrying out the commandments of Allah Ta'ala; name of a sahaabi.

غ

The Chapter Ghain

NAMES FOR BOYS

Ghaffaar غفّار
Allah's attribute meaning 'Most Forgiving'; 'Most Merciful'.
Name: Abdul-Ghaffaar.

Ghafoor غفُوْر
Allah's epithet meaning 'Most Forgiving'; 'Most Merciful'.
Name: Abdul-Ghafoor.

Ghulaam غُلام
Boy; servant.
Name: Ghulaamullah.

Ghanee غنِيّ
Prosperous; wealthy, independent; also an attribute of Allah.
Name: Abdul-Ghanee.

Ghauth غوْث
A title applied to saints and devotees who are continuously engaged in worshipping Allah Ta'ala. 'Ghauth' literally means a redresser of grievances or a helper or defender. In the light of this meaning, Allah Ta'ala is also 'Ghauth'.
Name usually kept is Ghulaam Ghauth.

Ghiyaath غِيَاث
Deliverance from hardships; redress; aid given in time of need.
An ideal combination: Ghiyaathud-deen.

NAMES FOR GIRLS

Ghazaalah غزَالة
A young deer; gazelle; the sun.

ف

The Chapter Faa

NAMES FOR BOYS

Faakhir فَاخِر
Excellent; precious; honourable.

Faarooq فَارُوْق
One who distinguishes between right and wrong; title of Umar (RA)

Faadhil فَاضِل
An accomplished person; virtue and knowledge.

Fattaah فَتَّاح
One who opens; one who attains victory; an attribute of Allah Ta'ala.
Name: Abdul-Fattaah.

Fath فَتْح
Victory; success; conquest; opening. Name: Fathe-Muhammad.

Fakhr فَخْر
Glory; a thing to be proud of.
Suitable combination: Fakhrud-Deen.

Farhaan فَرْحَان
Glad; joyful.
Suitable combination of names: Farhaan Ahmad and Farhaan Ali.

Furqaan فُرْقَان
A criterion (for distinguishing truth from falsehood). Another name for the Qur'aan since it distinguishes truth from falsehood.
Name: Furqaan Ahmad.

Fareed فَرِيْد
Singular; unique; precious; a precious pearl.
Name; Fareedud-Deen.

Fadhl فَضْل
Excellence; virtue; superiority; extra; grace; bounty; wisdom.
Good combination of names: Fadhlullaah, Fadhlur-Rahmaan. Fadhlud-Deen, Fadhl Ahmad, Fadhl Muhammad, Fadhlul-Kareem.

Fudhail فُضَيْل
Diminutive of *Fadhl*.

Faqeer فَقِيْر

One who leads a life of piety; one who renounces the world.
Suitable combinations: Faqeer Ahmad, Faqeer Muhammad, Faqeer Hasan.

Faheem فَهِيْم

Intelligent; learned.
Names: Faheemud-Deen, Faheem Ahamad.

Fu'aad فُؤَاد

The heart.

Faisal فَيْصَل

An impartial judge; an arbitrator.

Faidh فَيْض

Generosity; grace; favour; beneficience; abundance.
Names: Faidud-Deen, Faidh Ahmad.

Fay-yaadh فَيَّاض

One who confers great favours; most generous and bountiful.

Fu-yoodh فُيُوْض

Plural of *Faidh* meaning favours, bounties.
Name: Fu-yoodhur-Rahmaan.

NAMES FOR GIRLS

Faakhirah فَاخِرَة

Excellent; precious; honourable.

Faadhilah فَاضِلَة

An accomplished lady; surplus; knowledge and virtue.

Faatimah فَاطِمَة

The baby girl who is weaned; name of the beloved daughter of Rasoolullah *sallallaahu-alayhi-wasallam* and wife of Ali (RA).

Faa'izah فَائِزَة

Successful; prosperous; victorious.

Farhaanah فَرْحَانَة

Glad; joyful.

Farhat فَرْحَت

Delight; pleasure; joy.

Firdows فِرْدَوْس

A garden; paradise; a bed of roses.

Fareedah فَرِيْدَة

Unique; singular; precious.

Fadheelah فَضِيْلَة
Excellent; perfection, virtue; knowledge.

Fawziyah فَوْزِيَة
Victorious; successful; one who has attained salvation.

Faheemah فَهِيْمَة
Intelligent; learned.

Fay-yaadhah فَيَّاضَة
A lady who confers great favours; most generous and bountiful.

ق

The Chapter Qaaf

NAMES FOR BOYS

Qaadir قادر
Powerful; mighty; capable; an epithet applied to Allah Ta'ala. Name: Abdul-Qaadir.

Qaasim قاسم
One who distributes; name of the beloved son of Rasoolullah *sallal-laahu-alayhi-wasallam*; also his attribute.

Quddoos قدّوس
Holy; pure; free from any defects; an attribute of Allah Ta'ala. Name: Abdul-Quddoos.

Qadeer قدير
Powerful; mighty; an epithet exclusively applied to Allah Ta'ala. Name: Abdul-Qadeer.

Qutub قُطب
The fulcrum around which the mill-stone rotates; the leader on whom depends the affairs of the people; best; the northern star. Name: Qutbud-Deen.

Qamar قمر
The moon. Suitable combinations: Qamrul-Islaam, Qamrud-Deen. Suitable combination of names: Qamrul-Islaam and Qamrud-Deen.

Qawee قوى
Strong; powerful; firm; mighty; an attribute of Allah Ta'ala. Name: Abdul-Qawee.

Qay-yoom قيّوم
Everlasting; an epithet applied exclusively to Allah Ta'ala. Name: Abdul-Qayyoom.

Qudsiyyah, Qud-doo-siyyah قُدْسِيَّة ، قُدّوسِيَّة

A girl who is free from any physical or moral defects; a blessed girl; a pious girl; celestial.

Qamar قَمَر

The moon.

Name: Qamrun-Nisaa'.

ک

The Chapter Kaaf

NAMES FOR BOYS

Kaazim کَاظِم
One who suppresses his anger; strong; the title of Imaam Moosaa (RA), the son of Imaam Ja'far Saadiq (RA).

Kaamil کَامِل
Perfect; complete; total; learned.

Kabeer کَبِیر
Immense; great; senior; Allah's epithet.

Karaamat کَرَامَت
Generosity; magnificence; excellence; supernatural power.
Name: Karaamat Ali.

Karam کَرَم
Kindness; generosity; bounty; clemency.
Names: Karam Ali, Karam Ilaahee.

Kareem کَرِیم
Bountiful; magnificent; gracious; merciful; an attribute of Allah.
Name: Abdul-Kareem.

Kifaayat کِفَایَت
Abundance; self-sufficience.
Name: Kifaayatullah.

Kaleem کَلِیم
A speaker; when two persons are conversing with one another then the one is called "Kaleem" with respect to his fellow-speaker; *Kaleemullah* was the title of Sayyidona Moosaa (AS) since he conversed with Allah Ta'ala.

Kauthar کَوثَر
Name of a fountain in Jannah.

NAMES FOR GIRLS

Kaamilah كَامِلَة
Complete; perfect.

Kareemah كَرِيْمَة
A generous lady; bountiful; something invaluable.

Kulthoom كُلْثُوم
A lady with rosy, healthy cheeks; name of the beloved daughter of Rasoolullah *sallallaahu-alayhi-wasallam.*

Kauthar كَوْثَر
Name of a fountain in Jannah.

ل

The Chapter Laam

NAMES FOR BOYS

Laa'iq لائق
Worthy: deserving: capable: decent.
Names: Laa'iq Ahmad. Laa'iq Ali.

Lutf لطف
Kindness; courtesy; favour.
Name: Lutfur-Rahmaan.

Lateef لَطِيف
Delicious; agreeable; fine; delicate; courteous; elegant; benevolent: an epithet applied to Allah Ta'alaa.
Name: Abdul-Lateef.

Luqmaan لقمان
Name of a great sage, *hakeem* or prophet whose mention is made in the Holy Qur'aan. This word is sometimes used metaphorically for a wise, intelligent and experienced man.

Loot لُوط
Name of a great prophet of Allah Ta'ala.

La'eeq لِئيق
Worthy; capable; clever.

Liyaaqat لِياقت
Worth; capability; merit. Good combinations: Liyaaqat Ali/Ahmad.
Good combinations: Liyaaqat Ali, Liyaaqat Ahmad.

Laa'iqah لَائِقَة
Worthy; deserving; capable; decent.

Lubnaa لُبْنَى
A tree yielding a milk-like liquid which is even sweeter than honey.

Lateefah لَطِيْفَة
Pleasantry; humour.

Laylaa لَيْلَى
Name of the beloved mistress of Majnoon in the famous tales of *Laylaa Majnoon*; also the name of a lady sahaabi (RA).

م

The Chapter Meem

NAMES FOR BOYS

Maajid مَاجِد
Glorious; honourable; generous; Allah's attribute.
Names: Abdul-Maajid, Maajid Ali.

Maalik مَالِك
Master; lord; an epithet applied to Allah Ta'ala; name of a sahaabi.
Name: Abdul-Maalik.

Mubaarak مُبَارَك
Blessed; auspicious; august; fortunate.

Mobeen مُبِين
Manifest; clear; Rasoolullah's *sallallaahu-alayhi-wasallam* attribute.

Mateen مَتِين
Strong; solid; of resolute mind; The Prophet's attribute.
Names: Mateen Ahmad, Mateenud-Deen.

Mujtabaa مُجْتَبٰى
Elected; chosen; title of Rasoolullah *sallallaahu-alayhi-wasallam.*

Mujeeb مُجِيب
One who answers; one who accepts or grants something; Allah's epithet.
Name: Abdul-Mujeeb.

Majeed مَجِيد
Glorious; noble; exalted; an epithet of Allah Ta'ala.
Names: Abdul-Majeed, Majeedud-Deen.

Muhibb مُحِبّ
A lover; friend.
Names: Muhibbullah, Muhibbur-Rahmaan.

Mahboob مَحْبُوب
Beloved.
Mahboobur-Rahmaan, Mahboobul-Haqq, Mahboob-e-Ilaahee.

Muhsin مُحْسِن
Benefactor; benificient; one who confers favours.

Mahfooz مَحْفُوظ

Preserved; guarded; secure.

Name: Mahfoozur-Rahmaan.

Muhammad مُحَمَّد

The praised one; name of last prophet of Allah Ta'ala. May Allah Ta'ala shower his blessings upon him.

Mahmood مَحْمُود

Praiseworthy; elegant; attribute of Rasoolullah *sallallaahu-alayhi-wasallam.*

Muhyee مُحْيِى

One who gives and sustains life; one of the attributes of Allah Ta'ala Name: Muhiyyud-Deen.

Mukhtaar مُخْتَار

Selected; chosen; the most exquisite; one who acts with a free will: one who has the choice; invested with authority and power: attribute of Rasoolullah *sallallaahu-alayhi-wasallam*.

Names: Mukhtaar Ahmad/Husain.

Makhdoom مَخْدُوم

One who is held in reverence and served by others: lord; master.

Mud-dath-thir مُدَّثِّر

One who is enwrapped in cloth; an attribute of Rasoolullah *sallallaahu-alayhi-wasallam*; name of a *surah* in the Holy Qur'aan.

Muraad مُرَاد

Desire; intention.

Murtaadh مُرْتَاض

Disciplined; one who endeavours in worshipping Allah Ta'ala and in suppressing the desires of the *nafs* or *self.*

Murtadhaa مُرْتَضَى

Chosen; agreeable; acceptable; title of Ali *radhiyallaahu-anhu.*

Mirsab مِرْسَب

Prudent; wise; name of the sword of Rasoolullah *sallallaahu-alayhi-wasallam.*

Murshid مُرْشِد

An instructor; a guide.

Marghoob مَرْغُوب

Desired; desirable; pleasant.

Muzzammil مُزَّمِّل

One who is enwrapped in cloth; title of Rasoolullah *sallallaahu-alayhi-wasallam*; name of a *surah* in the Holy Qur'aan.

Mustafeedh مُسْتَفِيْض

Profitting; one who is desirous of gaining.

Names: Mustafeedhur-Rahmaan; Mustafeedhul-Hasan; Mustafeedh Ahmad.

Mas'ood مَسْعُوْد

Prosperous; happy; dutiful; obedient; fortunate; name of an illustrious sahaabi (RA).

Name: Mas'ood Ahmad.

Muslim مُسْلِم

One who professes Islaam; one who makes obeisance to the will of Allah Ta'alaa and Rasoolullah *sallallaahu-alayhi-wasallam*; name of a sahaabi (RA).

Names: Muslim Ahmad, Muhammad Muslim.

Maseeh مَسِيْح

One who is blessed with piety from the cradle to the grave; another name of Hadhrat Eesaa (AS).

Names: Maseehullah, Maseeh Ahmad.

Mushtaaq مُشْتَاق

Desirous of; yearning for; hopeful of.

Names: Mushtaaq Ahmad, Mushtaaq Ali.

Mashkoor مشكور

The person to whom one is indebted.

Name: Mashkoor Ahmad.

Mash-hood مَشْهُوْد

Present; manifest; The Day of Jumu'ah; The Day of Judgement; The Day of Arafah.

Misbaah مِصْبَاح

Lamp; lantern.

Names: Misbaahullah, Misbaahud-Deen, Misbaahul-Islaam.

Musad-diq مُصَدِّق

One who accepts another's word as truth.

Mustafaa مُصْطَفى

Chosen; title of Rasoolullah *sallallaahu-alayhi-wasallam.*

Muslih مُصْلِح

A reformer.

Name: Muslihud-Deen.

Muttalib مطّلب

Name of the grandfather of Rasoolullah *sallallaahu-alayhi-wasallam.*

Name: Abdul-Muttalib.

Matloob مَطْلُوْب

Desired; required.

Name: Matloobur-Rahmaan.

Mutee' مُطِيْع

Obedient; submissive.

Suitable combination of names: Mutee'ul-Haqq, Mutee'ullaah, Mutee'ur-Rahmaan.

Muzaffar مُظَفَّر

Victorious.

Name: Muzaffar Ahmad.

Mazhar مَظْهَر

A spectacle; sight; view.

Name: Mazhar Ali, Mazhar Husain.

Mu'aawiyah مُعَاوِيَة

A gallant lad; a powerful lad who overpower his opponent without difficulty; a leader who is able to assemble his subordinates by a single command; name of a Sahabi (RA).

Ma'roof مَعْرُوْف

Well-known; famous; noted.

Name: Muhammad Ma'roof.

Mu'izz مُعِز

One who bestows honour i.e. Allah Ta'ala.

Names: Abdul-Mu'izz, Mu'izzud-Deen.

Ma'soom مَعْصُوْم

Innocent; protected.

Names: Muhammad Ma'soom, Ma'soom Ahmad.

Mu'azzam مُعَظَّم

Honoured; exalted; revered.

Name: Mu'azzam Ali.

Mu'een مُعِيْن

A helper; an aide.

Names: Mu'eenud-Deen, Mu'eenul-Haqq.

Mughnee مُغْنِى

One who releases another from straitened circumstances; Allah's epithet.

Name: Abdul-Mughnee.

Miftaah مِفْتَاح

Key.

Names: Miftaahullah, Miftaahud-Deen.

Maqbool مَقْبُوْل
Chosen; accepted.
Names: Maqboolur-Rahmaan, Maqbool Husain, Maqbool Ahmad.

Muqtadir مُقْتَدِر
Powerful; mighty; Allah's attribute.
Name: Abdul-Muqtadir.

Muqsit مُقْسِط
Just; impartial; Allah's attribute.
Name: Abdul-Muqsit.

Maqsood مَقْصُوْد
Aim; object.
Name: Maqsood Ahmad.

Muqeet مُقِيْت
Provider; an attribute applied to Allah Ta'alaa.
Name: Abdul-Muqeet.

Mukarram مُكَرَّم
Venerable; noble; illustrious.

Malik مَلِك
King; an attribute applied to Allah Ta'alaa.
Name: Abdul-Malik.

Mumtaaz مُمْتَاز
Distinguished; illustrious; excellent.
Name: Mumtaaz Ahmad.

Mannaan مَنَّان
A great benefactor; an attribute applied to Allah Ta'alaa.
Name: Abdul-Mannaan.

Mansoor مَنْصُوْر
One who is given assistance; protected; triumphant.
Names: Mansoor Ahmad, Mansoorul-Haqq.

Mun'im مُنْعِم
Generous; benefactor; Allah's epithet.
Name: Abdul-Mun'im.

Munawwar مُنَوَّر
Brilliant; illuminated.
Name: Munawwar Ali.

Minhaaj مِنْهَاج
Way; road.
Name: Minhaajud-Deen.

Muneeb مُنِيْب

One who turns to Allah Ta'ala...seeking His pardon.
Names: Muneeb Ahmad, Muneebur-Rahmaan.

Muneer مُنِيْر

Splendid; shining; something that reflects light.

Moosaa (usually spelt Moosa) مُوْسٰى

Name of an illustrious prophet of Allah.

Mu'min مُؤمِن

A Believer; one who advocates peace and harmony; Allah's attribute
Name: Mu'min, Abdul-Mu'min.

Mahdee مَهْدِیْ

One who is guided rightly; name of an Imaam who will make his expected appearance before Qiyaamah; an attribute of Rasoolullah *sallallaahu-alayhi-wasallam.*

Muhaimin مُهَيْمِن

One who provides sanctuary from any hazard or danger; one who protects; one who is merciful; an attribute of Allah Ta'ala.
Name: Abdul-Muhaimin.

Maimoon مَيْمُوْن

Blessed; good fortune.

NAMES FOR GIRLS

Maajidah مَاجِدَة

Glorious; honourable; generous.

Maariyah مَارِيَة

A lady with fair complexion; name of one of the sacred wives of Rasoolullah *sallallaahu-alayhi-wasallam.*

Mubeenah مُبِيْنَة

Menifest; clear.

Mateenah مَتِيْنَة

Strong; solid; of resolute mind.

Mujeebah مُجِيْبَة

One who answers or grants something.

Majeedah مَجِيْدَة

Noble; exalted.

Mahmoodah مَحْمُوْدَة

Praiseworthy; praised; elegant.

Maryam مَرْيَم

Name of the mother of Sayyidona Easaa *alayhis-salaam* and daughter of Imraan *alayhis-salaam.*

Mas'oodah مَسْعُوْدَة

Happy; fortunate; prosperous; gracious; favourable; august.

Mash-hoodah مَشْهُوْدَة

Present; manifest.

Ma'soomah مَعْصُوْمَة

Innocent; protected.

Maleehah مَلِيْحَة

A beautiful and charming lady.

Mumtaaz مُمْتَاز

Distinguished; exalted.

Munaw-war مُنَوَّر

Brilliant; illuminated; full of light.

Muneebah مُنِيْبَة

One who turns towards Allah Ta'ala; one who repents.

Muneerah مُنِيْرَة

Brilliant; shining; something that reflects light.

Moonisah مُوْنِسَة

An intimate friend.

Mahdiyyah مَهْدِيَّة

A rightly-guided lady.

Mu'minah مُؤْمِنَة

A lady who believes or has *imaan* in Allah; a lady who offers peace and harmony.

Maimoonah مَيْمُوْنَة

Blessed; of good fortune.

ن

The Chapter Noon

NAMES FOR BOYS

Naasir نَاصِر
Helper; aide; defender.
Name: Naasir Ali.

Naazhim نَاظِم
Administrator; director; govenor; a composer of verses.
Name: Naazhimud-Deen.

Nabeel نَبِيْل
Handsome; intelligent; dexterous; one who is skilled in archery.

Nithaar نِثَار
To strew; to sacrifice.
Name: Nithaar Ahmad.

Najam نَجْم
Star; planet.
Names: Najmul-Islaam, Najmud-Deen.

Najeeb نَجِيْب
Excellent; noble; generous; praiseworthy.

Nadeem نَدِيْم
A companion; a courtier.

Nazar نَذْر
Charity; offering; vow; *sadaqah.*
Names: Nazrur-Rahmaan, Nazrul-Islaam.

Nazeer نَذِيْر
A warner; a courtier; title of Rasoolullah *sallallaahu-alayhi-wasallam.*
Name: Nazeer Ahmad.

Naseem نَسِيْم
Zephyr; a cool breeze; fragrant air.

Nasar نَصْر
Help; aid; support; name of a sahaabi *radhiyallaahu-anhu.*
Names: Nasrud-Deen, Nasrullah, Nasrul-Haqq.

Naseer نَصِيْر
A helper; a friend; name of a sahaabi *radhiyallaahu-anhu.*

Nizaam نِظَام
Order; system; a string of pearls.
Name: Nizaamud-Deen.

Nazheer نَظِيْر
Precedent; alike; equal to.
Names: Nazheer Ahmad, Nazheer Husain.

Nazheef نَظِيْف
Clean; neat; chaste.
Name: Nazheefud-Deen.

Nu'maan نُعْمَان
Name of Imaam Aboo Haneefah (RA).; also name of a sahaabi (RA)

Ni'mat نِعْمَت
Blessing; boon; grace; comforts of life.
Names: Ni'matullah, Ni'matur-Rahmaan.

Na'eem نَعِيْم
Pleasure; bounty; Jannah; anything given as gift; name of a sahaabi.

Nafees نَفِيْس
Refined; pure; choice; exquisite.

Nooh نُوْح
Name of prophet of Allah.

Noor نُوْر
Light; Allah's epithet.
Suitable names: Muhammad Noor, Noor Muhammad, Noor Ahmad, Noorud-Deen, Noorul-Haqq, Noorul-Islaam.

NAMES FOR GIRLS

Naajidah نَاجِدَة
Courageous; a lady who accomplishes difficult tasks.

Naadirah نَادِرَة
Rare; choice; precious.

Naasirah نَاصِرَة
Helper; aide; assistant.

Naadhirah نَاضِرَة
One with healthy and happy looks; a bright face reflecting lustre and *noor*.

Naafi'ah نَافِعَة
Profitable; advantageous; useful; beneficial; good.

Naa'irah نَائِرَة
Shining; glittering.
Naa'ilah نَائِلَة
Something worth acquiring; name of the wife of Uthmaan (RA).
Nabeelah نَبِيْلَة
Beautiful; intelligent; dexterous.
Najmus-Sahar نَجْمُ السَّحَر
The morning star.
Najmah نَجْمَة
Star; a fine species of grass.
Najeebah نَجِيْبَة
Excellent; noble; generous; praiseworthy.
Najeedah نَجِيْدَة
Brave; a lady who accomplishes difficult tasks.
Nadeemah نَدِيْمَة
A companion; friend.
Nazeerah نَذِيْرَة
Anything offered as a token of respect; anything given as sacrifice; a child who has been dedicated by his parents to serve Allah.
Narjis نَرْجِس
A flower resembling the eye; narcissus.
Nuzhat/Nuzhah نُزْهَت، نُزْهَة
Freshness; cheerfulness.
Nasreen نَسْرِيْن
A white rose; Jericho rose.
Naseelah نَسِيْلَة
Honey that flows from the comb.
Naseemah نَسِيْمَة
Zephyr; fragrant or cool breeze.
Ni-shaat نِشَاط
Cheerfulness; joy; sprightliness.
Nusrat نُصْرَت
Help; aid; support.
Naseerah نَصِيْرَة
A helper; friend; name of a shaabi lady (RA).
Nazeerah نَظِيْرَة
Alike; resembling; female head of a group.
Nazeefah نَظِيْفَة
Clean; neat; chaste.

Ni'mat نعمت
A gift or blessing from Allah Ta'ala; boon; grace; comforts of life.
Name: Ni'matul-Ain.

Na'eemah نعيمة
Ease; comfort; pleasure.

Naghmah نغمة
Melody; song

Nafeesah نفيسة
Refined; pure; choice; exquisite.

Nak-hat نكهت
Fragrance.

Noorun-Nisaa' نور النساء
The light of the ladies or the most beautiful among ladies.

Naheedah نهيدة
Soft butter; honourable; attractive.

Nay-yar نيّر
Luminous; shining.

و

The Chapter Waaw

NAMES FOR BOYS

Waajid وَاجِد
One whose wants are satisfied; one who endeavours; an inventor; wealthy; a lover or beloved.
Names: Waajid Ali, Waajid Husain.

Waahid وَاحِد
One; without partner; unique; an epithet applied to Allah Ta'ala.
Name: Abdul-Waahid.

Waasi' وَاسِع
Capacious; ample; one who possesses abundant (of anything); Allah's attribute meaning The All-Controlling.
Name: Abdul-Waasi'.

Wajaahat وَجَاهَت
Comeliness; dignity; elevated position.

Wajeeh وَجِيه
Of good and comely appearance.

Waheed وَحِيد
Unique; unparalleled.

Wadood وَدُود
Friend; companion; beloved; Allah's attribute.
Name: Abdul-Wadood

Wazeer وَزِير
An adviser or counsel to the king; one who renders a helping hand in some task.
Names: Wazeer Ahmad/Husain/Ali, Wazeerud-Deen.

Waseem وَسِيم
Beautiful; handsome.
Names: Waseemud-Deen, Waseem Ahmad.

Waqaar وَقَار
Dignity; modesty; constancy; mildness.
Names: Waqaar Ahmad/Husain, Waqaarul-Haqq, Waqaarud-Deen.

Wakeel وكيل
Counseller; attorney; agent; adroit; Allah's attribute.
Names: Abdul-Wakeel, Wakeel Ahmad.
Waleed وَلِيد
Boy; child; name of a sahaabi (RA).
Walee وَلِى
Prince; lord; friend; guardian; a beloved of Allah Ta'ala; Allah's attribute.
Walee Hasan, Walee Muhammad, Walee Ahmad, Abdul-Walee.
Wahab وَهب
Gift; name of a sahaabi (RA).
Names: Wahabullah, Wahabur-Rahmaan; Wahabul-Haqq.
Wahhaab وَهّاب
One who gives charity etc. abundantly; Allah's attribute.
Name: Abdul-Wahhaab.
Wahhaaj وَهّاج
Shining; illuminated.
Names: Wahhaajud-Deen, Wahhaj Ahmad.

NAMES FOR GIRLS

Waajidah وَاجِدَة
One who has achieved (her goal); one who endeavours; a lover or beloved.
Waahidah وَاحِدَة
One; unique.
Waheedah وَحِيْدَة
Unique; unparelleled.
Wardah وَرْدَة
Rose; rosy; deep red colour; brave.
Waseemah وَسِيْمَة
Feminine of Waseem meaning handsome of face; pretty; goodly; elegant.

ه

The Chapter Haa

NAMES FOR BOYS

Haadee هَادِى

Leader; guide; Allah's attribute.

Name: Abdul-Haadee.

Haaroon هَارُوْن

Chief; protector; guard; the wealth of the entire universe; name of an illustrious prophet of Allah Ta'ala. Haaroonur-Rasheed was the name of a Khaleefah in the Abbaasi dynasty.

Haashim هَاشِم

One who smashes or breaks anything to pieces. Rasoolullah's *sallallaahu-alayhi-wasallam* great grandfather was named as such because he had established a public kitchen when Meccah was severely hit by drought. He would purchase food from Syria and most generously distribute it among the Meccans. It is said that he used to have crushed bread added to gravy which was fed to the people. Hence the name.

Hidaayat هِدَايت

Guidance; righteousness; instruction.

Name: Hidaayatullah.

Hurairah هُرَيْرَة

Kitten. This name is usually used in combination with the word 'Aboo', as Aboo-Hurairah.

Hishaam هِشَام

Name of a sahaabi as well as a Khaleefah.

Hilaal هِلَال

The crescent of the first night of the lunar month.

NAMES FOR GIRLS

Haajarah هَاجَرَة
Name of the beloved mother of Ismaa'eel *alayhis-salaam.*
Haalah هَالَة
A crescent-shaped ear-ring; name of the sister of Hadhrat Khadeejah *radhiyallaahu-anhaa.*

ي

The Chapter Yaa

NAMES FOR BOYS

Yaaseen يَاسِيْن
Name of a *surah* in the Holy Qur'aan.
Names: Muhammad Yaaseen, Yaaseen Ahmad.

Yaameen يَامِيْن
Blessed; auspicious.
Name: Muhammad Yaameen.

Yahyaa يَحْيٰى
This is the imperfect tense of *hàyy* which means 'to live.' Thus, *Yahyaa* would mean 'will live.' Name of an illustrious prophet of Allah Ta'ala.

Yazeed يَزِيْد
Increasing; multiplying. Name of the son of Sayyidona Ameer Mu'aawiyah (RA).

Ya'qoob يَعْقُوْب
Name of an illustrious prophet of Allah Ta'ala. Father of Sayyidona Yoosuf (AS).

Yoosuf يُوْسُف
Name of a well-known prophet of Allah–son of Ya'qoob (AS).

Yoonus يُوْنُس
Name of an illustrious prophet of Allah Ta'ala.

NAMES FOR GIRLS

Yaasameen يَاسَمِيْن
A sweet-smelling flower called jasmin.